A BOY FROM

First published in 2005 by
WOODFIELD PUBLISHING
Bognor Regis, West Sussex, England
www.woodfieldpublishing.com

ISBN 1-903953-86-3

A Boy from Soho

My experiences before the war, during the Blitz and in Italy with the RASC

FRANK GIANOTTI

Woodfield

The Author, Italy 1944.

Contents

Introduction

On numerous occasions over the years when, in the company of my family or friends, past events have been discussed, I have described things that I have experienced during my lifetime. On many of these occasions somebody or another has been sufficiently interested to observe that my experiences have been most unusual. "Write a book about your life, Frank," they have urged. I never found time or the patience to do so. Then, at the age of 69, in the later stages of my retirement years and in the tranquillity of my home in peaceful Aldwick in West Sussex, I decided to make a start. Upon reflection it seemed to me that my life could be divided quite clearly into two parts and that I should concentrate on the first part – the thirty-year period from August 30th 1923 until July 25 1953. In the main these were hard years, particularly the six years of the Second World War – when the first priority was to survive.

Apart from my own personal experiences, many of which I believe to be unusual if not unique, these thirty years were a wonderful period in history which I shall describe as seen through my own eyes. When dialogue is introduced the words spoken, obviously, cannot be exact after so many years have passed but they will be reasonably accurate and will, I hope, serve to paint a better picture of the happenings described and perhaps make for more interesting reading.

All my experiences are real, clearly remembered by me, aided by notes from diaries etc. Some names of individuals, however, have been changed to avoid any possible embarrassment to persons still living should my story ever be widely read.

I am hopeful that what follows will be interesting, particularly to future generations of my family for whom it will also serve as part of our family records.

I was born in Middlesex Hospital, London, on August 30th 1923. My father, Oreste Gianotti, was an Italian immigrant who had travelled extensively and had worked in various parts of Europe, in India and in Argentina, before deciding to make his home in England. My mother, Emily Violet, was a Londoner. They met in the year 1920 in Lyons Corner House in the West End of London, where they both worked. My father was then employed as a chef, and my mother as a waitress. After their marriage they lived in a tiny flat in the Soho quarter of London where many Italians resided and where my father had friends.

My parents had married relatively late in life. My father was 46 years of age and my mother 34 when I was born. Prior to my arrival my mother had gone through the trauma of delivering a stillborn child. My own birth, therefore, was a more than joyous occasion for my parents.

I was registered at birth as Francesco Giacomo Gianotti but was always known thereafter as Frank James Gianotti. In August 1924 my parents took me to Italy and I was baptised in Borgo D'ale, the little village in which my father was born, not far from the City of Turin. My Godmother and Godfather were Maria and Pierino Mattio (my father's sister and her husband). On numerous occasions, when I was old enough to understand, my mother related the events of the day of my baptism to me. It had been a wonderful day on which my mother was overwhelmed by the great kindness and affection shown to her by my father's brothers and sisters and all the members of the family who had travelled from all parts of Northern Italy for the occasion. My godparents were described by her as a marvellous couple who had showered her with love and kindness. Although they did not speak English and my mother had no knowledge whatsoever of the Italian language a warm bond was swiftly formed between them. I, of course, was too young to have any recollection of what must have been a wonderful family celebration.

I was not to see my Italian family again for over 20 years when, due to the fortunes of war, I was able to locate them in Turin in early 1945 as a soldier in the invading British Army. This wonderful happening I will describe later in my story.

1. My Early Years

My parents lived in a small but pleasant apartment in Stephen Street, just off Tottenham Court Road in London's West End, for the first few years of their marriage. When a second child was expected they were obliged to seek more roomy accommodation. They eventually rented a flat, again in the West End of London, in a road then called Little Pulteney Street. This flat was in one of a group of apartment blocks populated by working class people, mainly poor, of many different nationalities. Apart from English families there were Italians, French, Greeks and others. The apartment was very dilapidated, in an old tenement building, and was intended by my parents to be just a temporary abode. My brother David was born there on 25th August 1927. A third son, my brother Edward, was born on 28th December 1928. My father was not highly paid but my family had the basic needs of life – we were reasonably well fed and clothed. There was, of course, no television and we had no washing or drying machine, no refrigerator, no electric iron. (My mother did her ironing with a heavy flat iron, heated on the gas, her hand protected by a thick woollen pad). In fact we had none of the things that are today accepted as essentials in every home. Our one luxury was the sound and music we could enjoy from our wireless set which was powered by a large and heavy accumulator battery which had to be carried frequently to a local shop for re-charging! My parents led a Spartan life and what little money was available was spent in caring for their three sons.

I started my education in St James' and St Peter's School (in Windmill Street) which was immediately adjacent to my home. The playground in front of the school was separated from the apartment blocks by a massive iron gate about ten feet high. This was always locked. As the alternative route to school meant a short walk through two streets the iron gate presented the morning challenge. All the boys who attended the school, aged up to ten years, would climb over the top and gingerly down the other side taking care to stay close to the nearside wall thus escaping detection by the school staff! It seems quite miraculous but, apart from the occasional piece of torn clothing left impaled on the spikes above the gate and the odd incidence of cuts and bruises, no serious injury was ever suffered by a child. The iron gate, however, remains in my memory always, perhaps psychologically representing one of the first of life's hurdles.

In the early 1930's, as a result of the great economic depression in Great Britain, my father, along with countless thousands, lost his job and had no regular employment for some years. This period was very grim, in fact a period of survival. My mother was wonderful, she would never allow heads to drop – assuring us that with God's help all would turn out for the better in due course. She took a job as a cleaner in the office of a Director of the Lex Garage which was almost opposite our residence and her earnings, plus what little my father received, kept the wolf from the door. I was now old enough to find ways of earning a little money. With one staunch friend, Stan Guest, I procured damaged fruit boxes in Covent Garden. We chopped these into small sticks and made bundles of firewood which we sold for fire lighting. Depending on size we obtained one penny or two pence per bundle! Stan and I also had the good fortune to share a curious evening job.

We worked for a few hours each week threading needles for a Mr Thompson – an elderly tailor. Mr Thompson was a kind old gentleman and after we had finished our work filling his racks with dozens of needles threaded to his weekly requirements he would provide us with a glass of lemonade and a fancy cake – a rare weekly treat.

I gave nearly all the proceeds from my various activities to my mother which helped a little with the family expenses. I often noticed how tired she looked but she never complained. My father also looked very tired and strained. I vowed that I would study hard, work hard, make something of my life and dreamt that one day I might become rich and take them on holiday to Italy.

During these years there was no money available for luxuries of any kind, consequently our leisure moments were occupied almost entirely doing things that cost nothing. Children played together in the local streets. Of the simple games that I recall one was 'Chipping'. This was a game for two players. A metal crinkly-edged bottle top was positioned in the middle of the road. Then each player, using a cord, alternately spun a top into the road – the top would whirl around at high speed, it was then picked up by placing the back of the hand on the road and transferring the spinning top to the palm of the hand via the first two fingers. It would continue spinning until the player banged it down onto the bottle top which would be sent flying. The winner would be the player who reached the opposite side of the road first. There were other games such as 'French Cricket' which was played with an old tennis ball and pieces of wood and, of course, when anybody produced a cricket bat we played what resembled a real game of cricket, using a fruit box as a wicket!

One of the venues for these activities was Archer Street – the narrow street at the back of the famous Windmill Theatre, suitable because there were high brick walls and not many windows to break and lorries and motor cars passed through only at intervals. Although there was great poverty this was never used as an excuse for crime. In the hard environment of the streets of Soho any minor offence by a child was dealt with firmly but fairly by the local policemen on the beat. A clip around the ear for a boy or girl who misbehaved was frequent and quite acceptable to their parents. The police force was widely respected. Annual holidays could rarely be afforded but whenever possible my parents took us for picnics in Green Park or to Putney Heath, or Richmond.

My mother had a sister (my Aunt Mil) who was married to an engine driver on the Great Western Railway (my Uncle George). They lived at West Acton in a cottage owned by the railway, directly above the central London railway line from London to Ealing. At the back of the cottage was a long garden from which one could watch the passing trains. My family was invited there every Christmas day together with another of my mother's sisters (my Aunt Alice), her husband (Jack), and their two daughters (Doris and Rene). It was the highlight of the year and always a joyous family occasion. Roast turkey, Christmas pudding, cakes, chocolates and treats that we rarely enjoyed were on our Christmas table in abundance. We played cards and board games and were in seventh heaven. West Acton is not far from Central London but to us children it was deemed to be 'in the country' – a clean and pleasant place, so different from our normal surroundings. I remember my aunts and uncles with great affection and thankfulness for their kindness on these and other occasions.

On rare occasions I was able to save enough money to afford a visit to the cinema. I have a vivid recollection of seeing 'KING KONG' at the London Coliseum, and the gigantic 'cut out' figure that was erected outside the cinema to publicise the film. It was a most thrilling experience for a young boy. We were in the year 1934. Film-making had made tremendous strides in just a few years and it was hard to believe that only seven years previously there was no such thing as a 'talking picture'. At about this time a young dance team, Fred Astaire and Ginger Rogers, appeared on the scene!

2. Sickness Strikes

To add to our family problems the year 1934 was to inflict a cruel blow. My youngest brother Edward (Ted as he was by now called) was a handsome child. His fair hair made him a striking contrast to David and me – both much darker. With his clear blue eyes he had an almost angelic appearance. The baby of the family, he was much loved by us and all who knew him. My parents had observed that he was not walking well, he had developed a limp that swiftly became more pronounced. The local doctor was concerned and referred him to specialists. After a series of tests a diagnosis was made. He had a tubercular hip and would need to be admitted to hospital for treatment. This might require him to remain a bed patient for a very long period with his leg encased in a metal frame. The prospect horrified us but there was no alternative. He became a patient at several hospitals and we were able to visit him at intervals as these were all within striking distance of London. During the long period away he was cared for by splendid doctors and dedicated nurses. He accepted his ordeal with calm and good humour. I rarely heard him utter a complaining word. He was sorely missed at home and there was a period of great sadness before we became accustomed to his absence. We prayed that his eventual recovery would be complete but over three years were to pass before he was finally cured.

3. A Painful Lesson

Despite all the family hardships, I enjoyed my schooldays immensely. In the main the teachers, men and women, were dedicated and kind. Willing pupils were greatly helped and I personally had no lack of motivation. Discipline was quite severe, however, and punishment for misdemeanours was frequent. The cane was regularly used on the hands, or on the rear end. I was not punished frequently but there were a few occasions – generally the result of boyish high spirits in the classroom. One event, however, is indelibly etched on my mind.

Every Friday we attended classes in woodwork. The teacher, Mr Thomas, was a very strange man, short and stocky with a square granite jaw, he had dark bushy eyebrows drooping over cold staring eyes. He had been a soldier in the 1914/1918 war and it was rumoured that his experiences in the trenches had affected him adversely. He would fly into a rage at the least provocation. On one particular Friday the class had been instructed to produce a simple piece of woodwork that required making two saw cuts about two inches apart and about half an inch deep. With the wood in a vice we were then required to gradually shave out the centre with a chisel, to produce a groove. I made the two saw cuts and, with the impatience of youth, placed the chisel at the side of the timber and gave it a hefty clout with a mallet – the section removed flew across the workshop! I might have got away with it but, to my horror, Mr Thomas had silently moved into a position directly behind me.

"What are you doing, boy?" he growled. "What the hell do you think you are doing?" Then his voice raised to a shrill frightening pitch. "You know damn well don't you, boy, that a piece of wood is a living thing and must be treated with respect?"

I was not going to argue.

"Yes Sir", I murmured, almost inaudibly.

"Place your hand on that workbench, boy", he ordered, "and look sharp!"

I complied.

Before I had time to blink I had received a crunching blow on the back of my hand with the mallet. The shock, as much as the pain from the blow, caused me to reel away from the bench.

"Now, boy, you know how that piece of wood felt", he hissed!

I think I was about to burst into tears but my friend Stan appeared.

"Don't cry Frank", he urged, "or the others will think you're a cissy."

I bit my lip and gave the departing Mr Thomas a long hateful look! I was just twelve years old but I had learned a painful lesson – it's generally easier to do things the right way but if you must ignore the rules don't get caught!

4. A Change of School

In the year 1935 I was required to change school and was enrolled at St Anne's School in Dean Street in the heart of Soho. I was at first very unsettled as I had great regard for the teachers at my first school and I had quite enjoyed the company of the friendly young girls in those junior mixed classrooms. I soon adjusted, however. The school was only about five minutes walk from home during which I would pass along Wardour Street, famous for its connection with the cinema industry, or alternatively along Old Compton Street where one could see the fascinating shops that catered for the immigrant population. I often stopped to cast an eye over the great variety of special foods on offer and to enjoy the tempting aromas from meats, cheeses and freshly brewed coffee. People always seemed to have time for a chat and a cheerful greeting and I became friendly with the shopkeepers who would occasionally offer me a fancy biscuit or a tasty piece of cheese. Soho had a marvellous atmosphere and people of many different nationalities lived in harmony together.

Being in the West End of London there was, of course, a fair amount of prostitution but the activities of these ladies was conducted in a much more restrained and less blatant manner that it is in the same area today. I got to know some of these girls by sight. Apart from the (often hideous) hardened old campaigners there were some very pretty, and very young, girls and I felt sorry for them.

I studied hard at school and also applied myself diligently to my homework. There were rather better facilities for sport at my new school and we were taken off to various parks and recreation grounds around central London for cricket and football. I developed a great love for cricket. It seemed to me to be a sport in which one could excel regardless of size. Despite my lack of height, being quick on my feet and with a good eye, I enjoyed considerable success with a bat and ball. I represented my school at both football and cricket.

At the end of term in April 1936 I delighted my parents with my school report. I had achieved first place in a class of thirty. My father rewarded me by the gift of a Meccano construction set. It cost sixteen shillings (80 pence today!) and, although I was aware of the economies that would inevitably have to be made to pay for this gift, I was overjoyed. In times when toys and games were not frequently available that set gave me and my brother David many hours of pleasure.

On the radio Bing Crosby was enjoying great popularity with songs like 'Lazybones'. Arsenal won the FA cup final. Harold Larwood was bowling like a demon on the county cricket grounds of England.

5. We Move to South London

In early August 1936 my family moved. We had been allocated a flat by the London County Council in a new block of flats in Poynders Road at Clapham South. The new accommodation, although modest, was a great improvement on our previous home. I liked the open spaces close to us – Clapham Common, Streatham Common and Wandsworth Common were quite near to us and the wide tree-lined streets all around us were vastly more pleasant than the narrow oppressive streets of Soho. We were very happy in our new environment.

I was swiftly enrolled at the elementary school in Bonneville Road, just a short distance away. I quickly settled into my new school and made friends.

My father had now been working for some time as a chef at the Royal Thames Yacht Club in Knightsbridge. He worked long hours, often arriving home in the early hours of the morning, and found the journeys to and from work exhausting. We saw very little of him at home, apart from the odd day off from work. He was not happy about Italy's position in the world. The Italians were in the final stages of their conquest of Abyssinia and, partly because of the sanctions unsuccessfully applied by Great Britain and other powers, Italy was becoming more closely allied to Germany and its evil dictatorship.

In Spain civil war began in July 1936. Under General Franco the insurgents fought bitter battles against the republican army. Italy and Germany sent great quantities of material aid to Franco. Later German planes carried out air attacks on Spanish cities, in particular the notorious savage attack by squadrons of planes on the old Basque town of Guernica resulting in the total destruction of the town and heavy loss of civilian life. The horrific nature of this bombardment was shown in newsreels at cinemas. In all these attacks a new type of aerial warfare was employed using 'Stuka' dive bombers which screamed down on the terrified population below. They would prove to be rehearsals for the massive air attacks that were later to be used throughout Europe in World War 2.

Just before Christmas David and I attended a party given by the Royal Thames Yacht Club for the children of members of staff. It was a wonderful day and we enjoyed delicacies that we had previously only dreamt about.

Christmas 1936 was a very happy time for my family. There was a little more money in the household and we could afford a few of the simple things that we had not previously enjoyed. Things were beginning to look up.

6. 1937

The year 1937 was memorable for me for many reasons. Edward the Eighth, the King who had reigned for less than a year, had abdicated at the end of the previous year following a bitter dispute with the establishment over his affair with Mrs Simpson. The date for the Coronation of the new King, Edward's brother George, was set for May 12th 1937 and on that date the Coronation of King George the Sixth and his wife Elizabeth took place.

The event was marked by great celebrations throughout the whole of Great Britain. In almost every road there were street parties and the singing and dancing went on long into the next day. I still have in my possession the printed programme for the entertainment provided by the residents of our particular blocks of flats on that joyous day.

In June 1937 the ex King married Mrs Simpson. I had by now firmly established myself at my new school and was very happy there. I achieved good examination results and looked forward to the prospect of taking up my place at a good secondary school at the end of the year. It was not to be. My father's health had deteriorated during the year and, with the reluctant approval of my parents I decided to leave school as soon as possible after the age of fourteen to obtain employment.

I was eager to obtain a job in the Post Office but, to my dismay, I was informed that, being the son of an Italian national, I was not eligible for employment by any Government department. I felt very angry about this situation, my mother was English, I had lived in England since birth and I could not understand why such a ruling could apply. It seemed so unjust. I had always considered myself to be totally English. My mother was concerned for me but not too worried. "Never mind, Frank", she said. "You'll soon find work somewhere else – and you will probably do rather better than working for the Post Office or the Civil Service." In October 1937 I obtained my first post as a messenger boy and general clerk with a small advertising agency in the West End of London. The offices were in Golden Cross House, directly opposite Charing Cross railway station. I travelled to my place of work by underground train and was paid the princely sum of fifteen shillings (75 pence) per week! I did not know it then but my mother would be proved to be absolutely right. I had taken my first step into the business of advertising, a field in which I would ultimately achieve a great deal of success. I was first, however, to experience many things of a very different nature over the next ten years or so.

7. The Death of Oreste Gianotti

In mid-December 1937 the family was devastated by the death of my father. I returned home from work one evening to be told by my mother that he had collapsed at home, having suffered an internal haemorrhage. He had been rushed to St James' Hospital in Balham where his condition was very grave. I comforted my mother as much as I was able to do and we prayed for him. The doctors were unable to save his life, however, and on the following day, December 15th 1937, he quietly passed away.

It was my first experience of death in the family and for the next few days I helped my mother to carry out the routine clerical duties that follow a death. The funeral took place a week later, just before Christmas. I remember it as the most painful and miserable Christmas of my life. I felt great regret that I had not been able to enjoy the company of my father for longer periods because of the nature of his work and the irregular hours he worked. I regretted also that I had not taken advantage of the opportunity to learn to converse with him in his native tongue, bearing the name Gianotti but being unable to speak one word of Italian.

I told myself that I must not look back. At fourteen years of age I was now the breadwinner and would take responsibility for looking after my mother and my brothers.

As soon as we entered the year 1938 I enrolled to take evening classes at the London County Council School at Tooting Bec. I studied on three evenings a week, after I returned home from work. I decided, initially, to study bookkeeping, arithmetic and English which were subjects I considered would be most useful to me. I knew that I must work hard if I was to achieve success in my life, particularly as my education had been so limited. Being poor provided great motivation!

The year 1938 passed fairly uneventfully with the exception of one dramatic event. At the end of September 1938 the Prime Minister, Mr Neville Chamberlain, had an historic meeting with Adolph Hitler, the German Chancellor, in Munich. He returned waving a piece of paper – a treaty between Great Britain and Germany, declaring 'Peace in our time'.

In Britain the agreement was welcomed with great relief but there was a feeling of shame that Czechoslovakia had been betrayed – sacrificed in the desire to avert a new world war. Many informed people were certain that the occupation of Czechoslovakia would not be the last conquest by Nazi Germany – there had only been a postponement of the inevitable.

I was kept much occupied with my studies and my work. I was intrigued by the advertising business and, during the course of my work, spent a fair amount of time in the offices and printing departments of the great national newspapers in Fleet Street. I marvelled at the speed at which newspapers were produced and spent every possible moment watching the great printing presses churning out the news. Occasionally when working late I could observe the very early editions being rushed to vans which delivered them to railway stations for despatch to all parts of Great Britain. One of the managers in the Advertising Department of the 'Daily Express', a Mr Maples, took an interest in me and gave me useful tips concerning his side of the business. I appreciated his kind advice and remember one observation very clearly. "Never," he said, "never underestimate the power of the written word." I did not fully appreciate the wisdom of these words until some years later.

At weekends I played cricket and football, depending on the season, and thoroughly enjoyed both sports. Whenever I could afford to do so I visited a local cinema, sometimes in the company of friends, or a local girlfriend. There we were transported briefly to a romantic world of make believe, all cares and worries temporarily forgotten.

In this period the 'cartoon film' reached a new peak with Disney's magnificent 'Snow White and the Seven Dwarfs'.

In mid-year 1939 I sat for my examinations set by the Royal Society for the encouragement of Arts Manufacturers and Commerce. I passed all three of my chosen subjects and my mother was delighted.

8. The Start of World War 2

On September 3rd 1939 I was at home with my mother in our first floor flat in Clapham. The dark clouds of war had been gathering for some time. Now, on this pleasant Sunday morning, we waited for the latest news on the ultimatum given by Great Britain to the German government. If Germany did not agree by 11 am to withdraw from Poland Britain would declare war, in accordance with our treaty arrangements with Poland.

We sat by our radio set hoping with all our hearts that Hitler would realise that, this time, Britain and her allies would be forced into war unless he acceded to their ultimatum. We prayed that there would be some way to avoid the horror of a Second World War.

It was not to be. At 11 am the Prime Minister, Mr Neville Chamberlain, announced in an historic radio broadcast that no reply had been received and, therefore, a state of war existed between Great Britain and Germany. Just a few minutes after, before we had even had time to absorb the news and to contemplate the awful consequences of a global war, the first air raid siren sounded. The hideous wail came as a frightening shock reaching, it seemed, into the pit of the stomach. We waited apprehensively for what we imagined would be our first air raid.

Then something occurred which would show me that there is humour to be found even in times of fear and tension. Our neighbours in the flat next door were an Irish couple – Mr and Mrs Clifford. Mrs Clifford was thin and angular, very excitable and vociferous, Mr Clifford, tall and thin, long-suffering and quietly tolerant. Both were very partial to a glass of whisky. Immediately the siren sounded I instinctively opened the front door and went out onto the balcony. There stood Mrs Clifford in a state of considerable agitation. "The bastards are here!" she shrieked, and then again, in a tone even more shrill, "the bastards are here!"

A glance at the skies and the absence of any aerial activity seemed to confirm that she was anticipating events somewhat! She continued with a torrent of devastating abuse directed at Adolph Hitler in particular and Germans in general. When, mercifully, she had exhausted herself the tirade ceased. She beseeched, "What shall we do? What shall we do?"

I noticed that she was clutching her gas mask in its cardboard box container and said, "I think, Mrs Clifford, that it would be a good idea if you sat down quietly indoors for a while, had a glass of scotch, and awaited events". I added, a trifle mischievously, "Perhaps it would be a wise precaution if you also put your mask on".

"I'll do just that", she replied, and swiftly re-entered her flat closely followed by Mr Clifford. He looked back at me and winked. "Thanks me darlin' boy", he said, clearly grateful for the prospect of at least a temporary respite from that rasping tongue!

Although this little event was, in retrospect, quite amusing it is worth recalling that all over Britain there were frightened people who, at the sound of that first siren, hastened to air raid shelters, underground stations and cellars, some even putting on their masks – terrified of the unknown.

In the event there was no air raid. We were informed in a subsequent radio broadcast that it had been a false alarm. Almost a year was to pass before the bombing of Britain would really begin.

I was just 16. On that same Sunday evening my mother remarked, "Well, Frank, at least you will never have to go to war". I nodded agreement; little knowing then how wrong this observation would prove to be.

9. The 'Phoney' War (and a Bicycle Ride)

The first six months after the declaration of war passed without undue hardship for my mother and me. My two brothers were evacuated from London. David went to Chichester, where he was well received by a most loving family. The head of the household, Mr Billinghurst, was a veteran soldier from World War 1 and the head gardener at Chichester Cathedral. He, and 'Mrs Bill', as she was affectionately known became a second mother and father to David and treated him as one of the family. His two daughters, of similar age to David, accepted him as a brother. Ted was sent to Selsey Bill, where he lived with many other children in a building previously used as a holiday camp. He also was well looked after by caring nursing staff and soon adjusted to his new environment.

I clearly recall how I established that all was well:- A short time after their departure my mother asked me if I would visit my brothers. I readily agreed. I had an old bicycle and set off from Clapham early one Friday morning (having obtained a day off from work). I pedalled hard through Surrey and Sussex, stopping just briefly to eat my lunch, and arrived in Chichester in the late afternoon. I was greeted in a very friendly fashion and was accommodated for the night in a spare bed in David's room. I was delighted to see how happy he was in his new home. Early the following morning I cycled to Selsey, accompanied by David, and established that Ted, also, was happy and in good health.

We returned to Chichester in time for lunch and, in the afternoon, I played with David for his school cricket team in a beautiful setting with Chichester Cathedral looming in the background.

On Sunday morning I set off for the journey home supplied with sandwiches and a bottle of fruit juice. I was very happy that my mission had been satisfactorily accomplished. I was less happy, however, after the first few hours had elapsed. The journey was a nightmare and one that I remember in detail. My bicycle developed faults and then, about halfway home, I had a puncture. Repairs delayed me for long periods and the journey seemed very long. It began to rain quite heavily. I battled on and reached the outskirts of Epsom when I had a puncture in the other wheel. By this time I was very tired after my weekend's exertions and, indeed, felt almost desperate. I wheeled my bicycle under the cover of a roadside bus shelter and sat down to gather strength.

Then, as has so often happened in my life in time of need, I had a stroke of luck. A touring cyclist, observing my plight, pulled off the road.

"Having a bit of bother old chap?" he remarked.

"Yes," I said, thinking that this was a considerable understatement.

"I had better give you a helping hand," he said.

There was no objection from me! He was obviously a very experienced cyclist and the repair was soon made. His destination was Brixton and he asked if I would like him to ride with me. I readily agreed. We pushed on until we reached Morden. The rain was now almost torrential and I suggested that we should take shelter and rest.

"No, old chap," he said, "keep going or you'll never make it".

I complied and carried on. I was well aware by now that my knight of the road was deliberately travelling at well below his normal pace and was chatting to me so that I would forget my weary body and the pain in my legs. We finally reached Clapham and he accompanied me to my home. I had been travelling since 9 am. It was now nearly 10 pm and I was barely able to stand!

"Would you like to come in for some supper?" I croaked.

"No, thank you," came the reply "I must get home… I start my army service tomorrow".

He shook my hand and, upon parting, remarked, "Remember, old chap, when you think you are spent there is always a little more in reserve – it's all a matter of willpower".

He mounted his bicycle and disappeared into the night. Although it was a relatively small event in my lifetime I never forgot that young man's kindness to a fellow traveller – a boy in need of help. Nor would I forget the wisdom of his message. My mother, who was more than a little concerned about me, was grateful that I had returned safely and was delighted to know that her two youngest sons were in good hands. (This was not so for a great number of children. Many returned home by Christmas 1939 because the expected bombing did not occur during the first months of the war. Others were desperately unhappy in environments totally foreign to them and were brought home by parents who considered that it was preferable for them to be with their families and face the consequences in cities that would have to suffer aerial bombardment).

The period to March 1940 passed quickly. Apart from some isolated cases, there was little enemy aerial activity. The war at sea, however, was a different matter. Many thousands of tons of British merchant vessels were being sunk at sea by the German 'U' boats.

There was a considerable reduction in supplies to Britain and rationing was controlled by the issue of ration cards. The cinema provided some relief. There were huge attendances at cinemas to enjoy films with stars such as Ginger Rogers and Fred Astaire, Ronald Colman, Cary Grant, Clark Gable, Spencer Tracy and, of course, the hilarious comedy duo Laurel and Hardy. In theatres Bud Flanagan and the Crazy Gang did much to lift public morale with their knockabout comedy and with songs so appropriate to the period.

10. The Blitz Begins

The spring of 1940 heralded a grim period. The German 'Blitzkrieg' began, ruthlessly employing large numbers of tanks and great mechanized armies backed by the overwhelming air superiority of the Luftwaffe. One after another great Countries were defeated. Denmark, Norway, Holland, Belgium and France were all conquered at lightening speed.

At the end of May and into the first week of June 1940 the British Armies were evacuated from Dunkirk. In operations unparalleled in naval history the Royal Navy, backed by thousands of vessels of every kind, achieved a miracle in bringing home over 330,000 men!

It would only be a matter of time before Hitler's attention would turn to Britain.

During this period I continued my daily office routine, travelling from Clapham South underground station to Piccadilly Circus. The office staff was reduced in number day by day. Executives were called up or volunteered for military service in the Army, Navy and the Royal Air Force. One commercial artist joined the London Fire Brigade and some of the girls joined the Land Army to help with food production.

My studies at evening classes were to be a great help to me at this time. It was obvious that the aim of my employers was to keep the agency going, if possible, and each remaining member of the staff would have to perform a variety of different tasks.

I had not yet reached 17 years of age and would not be called to military service for some time ahead. I would look after my mother for as long as possible and learn what I could about the business.

At weekends I played cricket. A good friend, Bernard Mattocks, was the son of a bus conductor who was the wicket keeper for a London Transport eleven playing at North Cheam in Surrey. He enlisted us both and we each achieved some success with bat and ball. We enjoyed many hours on those playing fields despite the background of war. All our fears vanished temporarily as we enjoyed the wonderful English game.

11. Italy Enters the War

On 10th June 1940 Italy declared war on Britain and France. My mother and I were deeply grieved at the news. She recalled how warmly she had been welcomed by my father's family during her visits to that beautiful country in the early 1920s and that when I had been taken there for my baptism in 1924 we had been welcomed everywhere by happy smiling people. She recalled, also, how my father's youngest brother, Davide, had been killed in 1918 in World War I, at 20 years of age, fighting against the Germans in the Italian Alps.

We did not believe that the Italian people had the desire for war and especially not for war with Great Britain. It seemed unbelievable to us that if my father had not died three years previously he would have been imprisoned as an 'enemy alien'![1]

My mother became afraid that we might suffer in some way because of the name we bore and one day asked: "Frank, do you think it might be advisable for us to change our name?"

"No mum, I don't," I said emphatically. "I am very proud of our family name and nothing will induce me to change it. My name is Gianotti."

At a later stage we took advice from friends and my mother was 'naturalized'. (She had assumed Italian nationality by virtue of marriage). What a farce, I thought, that a woman so entirely English, with a deep love of her country and unable to speak a single word of the Italian language should have to go through such a ridiculous rigmarole!

---

[1] It is interesting to record that many Italians were interned during the war, one of the most notable being Charles Forte – in later life to become Lord Forte, head of a great hotel and catering empire.

12. The Tragedy of the 'Arandora Star'

It had been decided by the Government to deport internees (described as 'enemy aliens') to Canada. A ship employed for this purpose was the 'Arandora Star'. Included with many internees – who in the main had no sympathy with Fascism or enthusiasm for the war – was an Italian Geneticist, Guido Pontecorvo. On July 2nd 1940 the 'Arandora Star' was torpedoed by a German U-boat. Many of the passengers and crew perished as the ship went to its watery grave. Only a few were rescued and survived. Pontecorvo was one of the fortunate few and ultimately achieved fame and received many honours for his work in the field of genetics.

It is interesting to recall that Pontecorvo's brother, Bruno, was a nuclear physicist involved in the development of the atom bomb in America.

I have often reflected that if my father had not died in 1937 he might well have been aboard the ill-fated 'Arandora Star'.

The sinking, in fact, was an event that persuaded the British Government to abandon its internment policy.

13. The Battle of Britain

The assault everybody had feared commenced in the middle of July. The Luftwaffe launched a savage assault on Britain. The initial attacks were carried out by large numbers of bombers and Stuka dive bombers, accompanied by fighter aircraft, and were directed at coastal ports and shipping convoys – mainly in the South East. Within days these attacks were shown on news films in cinemas and I marvelled at the courage of the young pilots of our Spitfires and Hurricanes, taking off time and time again to engage the German aircraft over the English Channel. I recall also the savage attacks by the Stuka dive bombers screaming down in almost vertical dives before releasing their bombs on the ships below.

In the middle of August 1940 the Luftwaffe switched the assault to the airfields in Southern England. These were heavily bombed and much damage was done to aircraft hangars, and to runways, also to aircraft on the ground. Again the RAF pilots were magnificent. Hundreds of enemy aircraft were shot down in aerial battles that could be seen from the ground all over Southern England. RAF losses were also heavy and it was widely feared that there might not be enough fighters and fighter pilots available to continue the battle much longer.

In September the German attack was switched to London and I had my first personal experience of war. Huge numbers of planes carried out air raids on the capital, culminating in the largest daylight raid on Sunday September 15th, a beautiful autumn day. I stood with friends in open spaces, spellbound as we watched the air battles above, squadrons of German planes being attacked by our fighters – many falling out of the sky to crash in violent bursts of smoke and flame. It was reported that 185 German aircraft were shot down on that fateful day. Certainly it was the turning point in the Battle of Britain.

I recall that fear was alleviated somewhat during this period by the exhilaration and excitement generated by the success of the RAF against the massed daylight raiders. The daylight attacks, however, were just the beginning. There was much suffering ahead for the British people…

14. Terror by Night

The nightly bombing of London which began on September 7th 1940 was carried out relentlessly for consecutive nights for the next two months! Although the bombing of London was to continue throughout the rest of the war, this was the period most frightening for me. I continued my daily journey to my office in the West End (by underground train from Clapham South station). At the end of each day I hurried to get home before dark. Inevitably, each evening, the air raid sirens sounded and the bombing began. Many citizens had by now decided to use the underground stations as a refuge at night, taking their mattresses and blankets and sleeping like cave dwellers on the station platforms. On the occasions when I was late getting home I literally had to climb over them to reach the escalator. It was painful to observe the awful conditions endured by these poor souls. I felt great pity for the elderly and the women and children in particular. What sort of an existence was this for them? The will to survive prevailed, however, and for many this was to become a nightly ritual, mostly borne with a spirit of comradeship and a great deal of humour.

Each day one would witness new evidence of the bombing carried out the night before. I had to make frequent journeys to various newspaper offices in Fleet Street. After one very heavy raid on London at the end of December 1940, when huge numbers of incendiary bombs were dropped, it was chilling to witness the appalling damage to the area of the City of London surrounding St Paul's Cathedral. Nearly every building was destroyed or damaged with St Paul's miraculously almost untouched, looming defiantly over the smoking ruins.

My mother and I decided to sleep in our flat and take a chance but there was a short period when we slept in an air raid shelter which had been built into the lawn area below. This was only just below ground level and would give protection against bomb blast and flying glass but not a direct hit. On one night, during a very heavy raid, our slumbers were violently interrupted by a sickening thud and a tremendous explosion. The shelter shook and clouds of dust came from the floor and ceiling. There were screams from terrified occupants. I feared that we had been hit but after just a few seconds could see that no damage had been done to the shelter. There was no panic and I reassured my mother that all was well, then cautiously emerged from the shelter accompanied by Mr Elms – a marvellous cockney character – together we peered across the road. Opposite had been a row of terraced houses. As the pall of smoke settled down we could see that a complete house had been destroyed. It was an extraordinary sight – a whole house removed just as you would cut a slice out of a cake. Mr Elms looked at me and, in hushed voice, gasped "Look at it Frankie boy – just like a bleeding toof's been taken aght!" The phrase was wonderfully descriptive. We picked our way through piles of debris to see what could be done but there was little hope of finding any survivors. The fire brigade and air raid wardens swiftly arrived to clear up the wreckage. I calculated that the house had been just 50 yards away – we had been that close to death! The memory of that night – the shock of the explosion and the choking feeling afterwards in that confined space – haunted me for a long period afterwards. We never slept in the shelter again, preferring to take a chance in the comfort of our own beds.

Apart from the demoralizing effect on the population, damage to buildings and railway stations was extensive. Many railway lines around London were hit and rail traffic was frequently disrupted. Repairs were soon made, in the most difficult circumstances. Heavy raids on many major towns and cities throughout Great Britain were also met with great courage and resolution and it was apparent that the people of Britain would not be beaten by the terror weapon of indiscriminate night bombing – no matter how long it would have to be endured.

15. The Bombing Continues

The first six months of 1941 presented a very depressing period for the people of Great Britain. There was very little good news: the bombing of all the big cities continued almost without respite. Night after night the air raid sirens sounded, swiftly the bombers arrived – the German planes clearly identifiable by the distinctive sound of their engines – and night erupted into a cacophony of terrifying sound. The ear shattering noise of the anti-aircraft guns, the shrill piercing whistle of falling bombs and the crashing sound of bombed buildings collapsing will remain forever in my memory.

I prayed for really bad weather which made enemy air attacks less likely and gave the blessed relief of an uninterrupted nights sleep.

In April the German army invaded the Balkans, swiftly overcoming Yugoslavia and Greece – where a small British army of reinforcement had only recently been landed. These troops then had to be evacuated to the island of Crete.

On May 20th 1941 Crete was attacked. In the initial onslaught about 3,000 German parachute troops were dropped upon the island in an operation later acknowledged as being one of the most daring and spectacular feats in military history. Once the Maleme airfield had been captured another 20,000 German troops were flown in by troop carriers or gliders.

The British troops fought heroically but were ill-equipped and were swiftly overcome. Worse was to follow – in the subsequent evacuation of the remains of our army (about 16,000 troops were rescued) the Royal Navy suffered terrible losses; three cruisers and six destroyers were sunk and many others badly damaged, including two battleships and an aircraft carrier, and the Navy lost over 2,000 men. Also, back in April the British armies had been defeated in Cyrenaica in North Africa. It was to me, still not 18 years of age, an awful period. It was difficult to imagine when the war would ever finish, and how it could possibly end in victory. The appalling prospect of victory for the Nazis and Fascists was too horrible to contemplate.

My mother was marvellous and an inspiration to me. "Keep your faith in God, Frank", she said, "the forces of evil will not triumph in the end". I was thankful that she was not alone during these, the darkest days of the war. Thankful that I was able to be at home to share the nightly ordeal but apprehensive as to how she would cope alone when I would eventually become old enough for military service.

16. The Germans Invade Russia

On the morning of Sunday June 22nd 1941 I turned on my radio to hear a news broadcast. What I heard was hardly believable – the Germans had launched an all out attack on Russia! I called excitedly to my mother "Come quickly mum, I think that, at last, this may be the news for which we've been waiting". We jumped for joy and embraced. From an almost impossible position there was now real cause for hope.

It seemed to me, instantly, that perhaps at last the Germans had bitten off more than they could chew, and, at least, their huge involvement on another front might mean that we would have some relief on our beleaguered island.

The greatest land battle in the history of warfare had begun! In the first stages of this new invasion the German armies, supported by the German Airforce and employing their ruthless 'Blitzkreig' technique, surged into Russia on a huge front extending from Lithuania, Estonia and Latvia in the north down to Odessa on the Black Sea. We listened to the radio frequently, eager for every item of news. Initially the news was not good – the German Army made huge advances into Soviet territory and by the beginning of September 1941 was deep into Russia and approaching Leningrad and Moscow. The reports coming from Russia described a campaign of great ferocity with the Russian people enduring the most appalling hardships. Millions died and the Russian Army suffered massive losses in troops killed or taken prisoner.

The battle for Moscow was delayed and did not begin until early October – then the Russian winter intervened. The heavy snows that followed and the bitter cold were conditions for which the Germans, strangely, were ill-prepared and, although they actually reached the suburbs of Moscow by the end of November, there was to be no further advance. The Russian General Zhukov had held back huge numbers of troops from the east, specially trained and equipped for warfare in Arctic conditions. On December 6th Zhukov unleashed his Siberians and achieved a great victory over the German army.

The Russian campaign caused suffering to both sides on a scale unparalleled in history but to the people of Britain it was seen as the turning of the tide.

At about this time my friend Bernard Mattocks volunteered for service in the Royal Air Force and commenced training for air crew duty. I would miss him greatly and I prayed that he would not be thrust into combat duties too quickly.

17. Frank the Firewatcher

In the last months of 1941, having now reached 18 years of age, I was required to remain in my office building all night whenever my name appeared on a roster displayed in the building, for the duty of 'Firewatching' shared with others employed in the same block. We worked in shifts. Whenever the air raid sirens sounded it was the task of the one on duty to be available to be on the roof of the building to sound a warning or to deal with any incendiary bombs that might fall. Sandbags and a shovel were placed on the roof for this purpose and we were also issued with steel helmets.

My office was situated in a corner building in Warwick Street, just behind Regent Street in the West End of London. The roof was six floors up and there was a small wall around the edge of the roof. I have always had a great fear of heights and I did not enjoy the occasions on which I trod that roof during a raid. The fierce glare of the searchlights, the thunderous noise of the barrage fired by anti-aircraft guns, the whistle of falling bombs and the explosions that followed, plus the constant danger of being struck by jagged pieces of falling shrapnel from the guns, all combined to make each exposed rooftop experience a nightmare for me. I retreated frequently to the relative security of the basement where Emily, a little cockney caretaker carried out her duties which consisted mainly of tending the coke-fuelled boiler heating the building. Emily was very grey, tiny, old, and had a wrinkled leathery face and an altogether 'witch-like' appearance but she was very kind and had a great sense of humour. She always greeted me warmly and provided a continuous supply of mugs of sweet hot tea. I became quite fond of her. "When will you be called up?" she asked one night, adding "you might be better off in the bleedin' army!" I didn't know the answer to her question but was inclined to agree with her observation.

I was thankful that I was not involved in firewatching duties a year or so earlier when the air raids were at their heaviest. When I felt depressed by the bombing, the shortage of clothing and the strict rationing of food I reminded myself that the suffering endured in Britain was not so great as the awful privations being inflicted on the conquered peoples of Europe and parts of Russia.

By arrangement the company offices were now shared with two partners in a small company producing synthetic food products – they had a female secretary who was ever present in the office and attended to the telephone. (One of the partners, a Mr James Collins, referred to as 'JC', impressed me greatly as a very enterprising and innovative businessman. He had great ideas for future business and took me into his confidence. I did not know it then but this man was to have a great influence on my life in later years). This company's lines were produced at a factory in Kilburn and I was able to obtain orders for large quantities of bottle labels for which I organised the design and printing.

During this period our own office staff had been reduced to two – myself and the father of the two brothers that owned the business. He attended the office only at irregular intervals to sign cheques etc and to pay me my salary. I placed advertisements for the few clients that we had, wrote any advertising 'copy' required, kept some simple account books up to date, had regular contact with clients, and even delivered 'copy' and printing blocks to the newspapers myself! I was in touch with an artist who had been a member of the staff and was now a fireman stationed in Lewisham in South East London. When I required any artwork for advertisements I travelled to the fire station and arranged for him to produce drawings in his off-duty periods. I was now tackling tasks for which I had received little or no training, learning as I went along. I found the challenge very exciting and I knew that the knowledge I was acquiring, in very difficult conditions, would stand me in good stead when the world eventually returned to normal.

18. The USA Enters the War

The two years of war that Britain had so far endured had been long and hard. Although America was sympathetic towards Britain, and had supplied us with ships and vast quantities of arms and equipment, the Americans had managed to remain neutral.

There had been some considerable tension between America and Japan over President Roosevelt's placing of an embargo on the supply of oil to Japan and the freezing of Japanese assets in the United States, following the American demand the previous July that Japanese troops should be withdrawn from what had been French Indo-China. What followed, however, was totally unexpected.

On Sunday morning December 7th 1941 a huge Japanese naval force, including six aircraft-carriers, delivered a massive surprise attack on Pearl Harbour, the great American naval base in the east Pacific ocean. Taken completely by surprise the American fleet was savagely bombed by over three hundred Japanese aircraft. Four battleships were sunk, three others damaged, and the American casualties on the ground were heavy. In just a little more than one hour the Japanese had assumed mastery in the Pacific and prepared the way for invasion by sea of British, American and Dutch territories throughout the region, including the conquest of Singapore.

The actual declaration of war against America by Japan was delayed until after the attack on Pearl Harbour had been carried out and, to the amazement of many, Germany also declared war on the USA.

There had been strong isolationist views held by powerful groups in America and had Germany's decision to declare war not been made there is little doubt that the Americans would have given the war in the Far East first priority. In fact it now became the declared policy of the USA to give priority to the war in Europe. The full weight of the great American nation would be thrown into the war.

In Britain there was great relief – at last all the forces of the free world were allied together.

My dear mother was elated at these momentous happenings, although painfully aware that millions more would die in the new theatres of war. "There you are Frank", she said, "you won't be needed after all – it will soon be all over now the Americans are in". Poor darling mother – she had no idea of the magnitude of the tasks ahead – but I was grateful that for the moment she would enjoy some temporary relief and relax in the sunshine of her sublime optimism.

19. I Join the Army

The letter I had been expecting for some time finally arrived. It contained my invitation to join the army. It was an offer I could not refuse! I had considered volunteering for military service on a number of occasions but had not done so mainly because I was fearful of my dear mother being left alone. Now the moment had come when I would have to go. I had very mixed feelings – apprehension about how I would adapt to army life but also a certain excitement and a feeling of satisfaction – I would now be making my little contribution to the war effort. Following a medical examination at Lambeth Town Hall I was to report to Durran Hill training camp in Carlisle on October 15th 1942. I informed my employer who was now to be almost alone in keeping the agency going.

When the day for my departure came my mother walked with me to the underground station at Clapham South. She did her best to hide her feelings but could not control the tears when I embraced her and said goodbye, promising that I would write regularly. I took the underground train to Kings Cross Station in good time for the connection for my journey to the north of England.

The journey was long and I had ample time to relax and think. I was just nineteen years of age but although small was fairly fit. I wondered how demanding the physical side of army life would be and especially how I would endure the training.

Periodically I thought back, sadly, to leaving my mother and I had a vision of that tiny woman returning home alone.

As the train chugged on I gazed at intervals, through closed windows, at the surrounding countryside. It was now becoming very cold and it began to rain. The train passed close to the Pennine Chain and the dark slopes of the mountains looked stark and depressing, matching my mood. I was very glad when the journey was over and the train pulled in to Carlisle station. I asked the stationmaster for directions to the camp. "A couple of lads just ahead are going there", he said, "hurry and you'll catch them up". I hurried on and caught up with two young men. "Allo lad", said one in a friendly Northern voice "we're off for a glass of ale before we report. Cum wie us". I joined them readily. There was a very pleasant pub quite near the camp and we had a few beers together. I had felt rather alone and meeting young men in the same boat as myself was a great relief.

We eventually reached the camp in the late evening. It was just as I imagined a training camp would be, with a large barrack square and numerous huts scattered around. We were enrolled swiftly on arrival and taken to a mess hall for a hot meal. It wasn't home cooking but very welcome nevertheless. Afterwards we were taken together by a corporal to a large hut which was to be our home for the next eight weeks. We were each issued with a palliasse (a straw-filled mattress) and three blankets. "You'll draw all your other gear tomorrow", said the Corporal. The beds were wooden and solid and the hut was cold. One of the soldiers already installed glanced at me and remarked "not the bloody Ritz is it mate?". He was too right! I made my bed and got between the blankets. I was by now very tired and slept well that night despite the unaccustomed conditions. My army life had begun.

20. Army Training Begins

At 6 am all hell was let loose – bugles sounding reveille and an NCO running along the barrack room crashing a stick against each bed to create maximum shock. "Get up you lazy sods! Mummy's not bringing you tea in bed this morning! Move yourselves! Breakfast in 30 minutes!"

The washrooms – so called – consisted of an outdoor shed in which there was a line of taps below each of which stood a bowl. The water was cold and shaving and washing was rather less than pleasant! At about 6.30 am we hurried to the mess hall for our first army breakfast. Hot porridge and steaming hot tea. Very welcome, especially as Carlisle was much colder than the south of England and we were in the second half of October.

The rest of the day was mainly taken up with lectures on what would happen during the next eight weeks of training, which would be carried out by Officers and NCOs of the Durham Light Infantry, and by the issue of Army clothing, boots, and kit. Being small I had considerable difficulty in obtaining clothes that fitted. That afternoon, in the barrack rooms, after having got to know some of my fellow recruits, I put on my long woollen army pants and found that the bottoms could be turned up by about six inches! There was another lad who was carrying out the same exercise. Both naked from the waist up we simultaneously bounded onto one of the beds and faced each other, assuming the posture of old-time prize-fighters. "Look!" shouted one of the others, "look at the great 'G' in his John LL's!" The assembled rookies exploded in a great roar of laughter. It was the first breaking of the ice in our new environment. The description applied to me at that moment stuck and for much of my army life I was to be known as 'The Great G'.

One of the young men I had met at Carlisle station, Wilf Raisbeck, was an ex-miner from Spennymoor, in County Durham, a big powerful man but with a very gentle nature. We formed an immediate friendship. That evening we were free to leave camp. Wilfred and I travelled into Carlisle together with two others. We explored the town and then found a pub where we chatted for an hour or so. It was fascinating for me to be with men from such different backgrounds and I found Wilf's soft Geordie accent most appealing. I felt strange wearing army clothes and the steel-tipped boots seemed to weigh a ton! I wondered how I would fare when the marching began.

We returned to camp at a reasonable hour, knowing that the following day the real business of being transformed from civilian to soldier would begin and that life would get tougher.

It was on the first morning on the barrack square that I made the acquaintance of the legendary Sergeant Major. The platoon was formed up in three ranks for an initial inspection. Tall and straight as a ramrod, with waxed moustache, he wore his peak cap so that his steely eyes were barely visible. As he moved between the ranks he came to a halt directly behind me. He stood so close that I could feel his breath on my neck. I flinched, almost imperceptibly.

"Don't move lad", he roared, "don't bloody well move when you are standing to attention!" He moved on, inspecting each soldier closely, and then returned to face the platoon. He addressed the corporal by his side.

"What a bloody shower!" he groaned. "We must have reached the bottom of the barrel! Wait until Hitler hears about this lot – he'll be overjoyed! They're scruffy and they are not fit.

Take 'em away and get each man a real haircut – then start making soldiers out of them".

He strode off muttering to himself. I reflected that this was a man to avoid if at all possible.

The infantry training began immediately, initially with long periods of 'square-bashing'. Training designed to make each man forget his individuality and become part of a team, to react speedily to word of command. The pounding of boots on the barrack square jarred the body and made the feet sore but I soon became accustomed to the ritual drill. There was no let-up, as one period of training finished another started. We were given periods of weapon training. Each man was issued with a 303 rifle but was also given detailed training on the use of Bren and Sten guns, other machine guns and the use of hand grenades which were thrown 'live'. There were also periods where we trained wearing our gas masks. Anybody who has experienced this, running over distances with a pack on the back for good measure, will tell you that this is a very unpleasant business.

The route marches were hard, increasing in distance on each occasion, although one could obtain some relief by enjoying the very pleasant countryside around Carlisle – when not marching in pouring rain!

There were times when I felt more dead than alive but as time went on I became aware that I was becoming much fitter and things did not seem so bad. There were also good periods allowed for physical training and sport and I enjoyed some splendid games of football.

When we were not detailed for guard duty or any other chore the evenings were spent mainly in the NAAFI canteen where one could pass the time quite pleasantly playing cards or enjoying a game of darts. Initially most men were too exhausted to travel into Carlisle but later, as we became more adjusted to the rigours of army life, Wilf and I made periodic journeys. On one of these we met a couple of attractive local girls and spent some pleasant evenings in their company and visiting their homes. These occasions were richly enjoyable after the hard routine of camp life.

As our eight weeks of training came gradually nearer to a close we carried out various field exercises and night manoeuvres. These were physically very demanding. It was now late November and the weather was awful. For long spells I was wet, cold and totally miserable. I had learned how to fight and how to kill but I fervently hoped that, when the eight weeks training course was completed, I would not be posted to an infantry unit.

During this period of training radio broadcasts to the nation by the BBC announced the news from North Africa of a great victory over the German army by the Eighth Army, under the command of General Bernard Montgomery, at the battle of El Alamein. Large numbers of German troops had been killed and it was reported that some 10,000 German and 20,000 Italian troops had been taken prisoner. A huge number of tanks and over 1,000 guns were also reported to have been captured. After years of military defeats and setbacks the news came as a tremendous relief and morale booster to the British people and to allied forces everywhere. There was a new optimism and a feeling that this victory could represent the turning of the tide.

21. I Join the RASC

During our infantry training we had been informed that when it was over each man would be individually assessed and posted to a unit of the army to which he was most suited. "We don't want square pegs in round holes", we were advised. "Each one of you will be posted to wherever your particular skills can be properly utilised".

Accordingly, at the finish of the training course, I was interviewed by an officer. "You have done very well in training" he informed me, "and you have scored high marks in the various intelligence and educational tests you have been given. I imagine you might well be very useful in, say, the Royal Corps of Signals". I felt flattered and was rather pleased. A few days later our individual postings were announced. My friend Wilf was to go to an infantry outfit and, to my utter amazement, I was to be posted to the Royal Army Service Corps to become a driver! I had never driven nor did I have any mechanical aptitude. I had never even sat at the wheel of a motor car or a vehicle of any kind. I felt that I would be the squarest peg in the roundest hole ever!

The army needed huge numbers of drivers, however, and I soon adjusted to my new situation, realising that whatever was ahead would be better than footslogging in the infantry. In due course I was transferred to the Royal Army Service Corps (also in Carlisle) for another six weeks course of training.

I was very sad to have to part company with my friend Wilf but I knew full well that this was an inevitable part of army life. We had a very lively night out together in Carlisle with our girlfriends and said our goodbyes.

When I arrived at my new unit the training commenced immediately. After a brief period of instruction I found myself at the wheel of a 3-ton truck, accompanied by a Sergeant instructor. The vehicle seemed gigantic to me and it was something of a gymnastic feat even to climb up into the cab. Being short I also had some difficulty in reaching the accelerator, footbrake and clutch. This was soon rectified by using a rolled up overcoat behind me, to serve as a cushion. I was quite surprised at the very short time needed for me to accustom myself to truck driving. In just days I was quite comfortable at the wheel. The driving instruction was helped greatly by an excellent course of vehicle maintenance and mechanical instruction during which I learned that each driver would be responsible for the maintenance of his own vehicle. Maintenance was carried out on the basis of a 16-day 'task' system. On each day one part of the vehicle would be checked according to rules laid down so that every part would be thoroughly inspected. After sixteen days the process would begin again. In the event of any malfunction, or need for repairs, army workshops would take over. The course was very thorough. As soon as drivers became proficient we were taken out together forming 'convoys', escorted by despatch riders on motorcycles. I experienced a sense of excitement as the huge trucks rumbled through country lanes and villages. My office desk seemed far, far away!

In mid January 1943 I passed my driving test. I was now Driver Gianotti (instead of 'Private') and when the six weeks were up I eagerly awaited a posting to my first unit. I was now anxious to get on with playing my tiny part in the prosecution of the war.

22. Back to London

The posting for which I had been waiting soon came. To my delight, and amazement, I learned that, together with a few other drivers with whom I had trained I was to be sent to a mixed transport unit in Kensington, West London.

We made the journey down to London by train and reported to our unit, housed in some requisitioned hotels in Gloucester Road. My own particular home was to be the Milton Court Hotel where I shared a large room with three other soldiers. We had wooden beds, with blankets and although the accommodation was now hardly luxurious we had hot water in which to wash and a roof over our heads.

There were large numbers of vehicles of every kind parked in adjacent squares and I was allocated a 3-ton truck for which I would be responsible. I was overjoyed at my good fortune, particularly as I knew that I would almost certainly have some off-duty periods in which I would be able to see my mother. I could hardly believe my good luck. A further bonus was the discovery that a fair proportion of the drivers were females, members of the ATS. These were mainly young girls, some very pretty, and as they were all billeted together in one of the hotels quite nearby, there was the agreeable prospect of some pleasant female company. In the event, however, there was not a great deal of spare time. My truck was in daily use as I carried supplies from depots in and around London to various military establishments all around the capital. The air raids were now less frequent which for me was just as well as the loads carried sometimes consisted of high explosives – including anti-aircraft shells delivered to batteries all over London. My duties as a driver were interrupted periodically by guard duties and some training courses – the army had by now decided that every soldier, whether driver, clerk, or cook, would be permanently ready for combat.

I managed to get home on a few occasions, sometimes on a 24-hour pass and periodically in my truck if I happened to be in the vicinity of my home. On all these occasions my mother was overjoyed to see me and I was very relieved to see that she looked reasonably well despite the harsh conditions.

On a few occasions, together with my friends in the unit and some of the ATS girls, I enjoyed some lively evenings in central London which was easily accessible by using the underground railway from Gloucester Road. The pubs were always packed to capacity by troops from many nations – Americans, Free French, Australians, New Zealanders and others – as well as civilians. It required some considerable effort to reach the bar and order drinks but the beer and spirits flowed freely nevertheless, usually in a foul smoke-filled atmosphere. There was music and singing and the terrible war going on all over the world was momentarily forgotten.

23. Horror at Buckhurst Hill

Although I had no burning desire for promotion I had, apparently, carried out my army duties satisfactorily and I was promoted to the rank of Lance Corporal. It was in this capacity that I found myself, away from my Company on detachment, in charge of a small unit (five drivers and myself) operating six trucks from a requisitioned semi-derelict house in Buckhurst Hill in Essex, not too far from London. Our task was to move military supplies, mainly in areas east of London and in dock areas along the River Thames. Each evening we returned to our billet where we slept in reasonable comfort on wooden beds with straw palliasses and blankets.

We decided on one particular pay day that we would all go out together that evening for a few beers at a local pub and, accordingly, gathered together after our vehicles had all arrived back at the house and had been parked for the night. I noticed that one of the men, Driver Childs (who, incidentally, had married a few weeks earlier), was not present. Observing his vehicle in its parking space, I enquired, "Where is Childs? He is normally at the front of the line when there's a beer on offer."

One of the lads piped up.

"He isn't feeling too great and has decided to stay in and bed down early. He spilt oil or fluid over his battledress doing some maintenance and he's a bit fed up about it but he's all right".

It seemed to be nothing out of the ordinary and, giving the matter no further thought, we made our way on foot to the local. The evening passed very pleasantly and we relaxed, enjoying a few pints and some jolly conversation. At about eleven o'clock we strolled back to the house and made our way to our rooms. Childs was sleeping in a very small room, on his own, and I checked to see if he was awake. The room was in complete darkness and he seemed to be sound asleep. By now I was very weary and got into bed. I did not know how long I had slept but I was awakened violently by the sounds of the door of the room being crashed open and loud anguished groans from somebody obviously in an acute state of distress. I was alarmed, jumped out of bed and switched on the light. What I beheld was a profound shock to me; Childs was standing in front of me. He was shivering and his eyes were swollen and inflamed.

"Look," he croaked.

He lifted up his vest and I was horrified by what I saw. His testicles and the surrounding area were blistered and bright red. "Help me for God's sake," he implored.

By now one of the other men had entered the room, awakened by the commotion. "Stay here and look after him," I urged, putting on my clothes as I spoke. "I'll get a truck out and rush him to hospital".

Within minutes we were on our way. I knew where the local hospital was situated and, with my heart pounding, drove like a demon through the darkness of the night. During the frenzied journey Childs said little except to groan occasionally. He did, however, manage to convey to me that he had been doing maintenance on some waste ground (often used by military people) and had found a jar which he intended to use to contain distilled water. He had opened it by holding it between his legs and forcing out the stopper and a liquid had gushed out over his legs and battledress. I did my best to assure him that all would soon be well. I glanced at my watch – it was 2.30 am. As I reached the hospital I quickly found the casualty department. I ran from the truck and requested urgent help.

Within minutes Childs was in a casualty bay receiving attention. I was not allowed to accompany him and waited anxiously outside. After what seemed a very long time a doctor came out to see me and asked questions. I told him everything that I knew.

He looked serious.

"I think he is suffering from exposure to Mustard Gas," he said. "The effects would not have been immediately visible at the time of contamination but were obviously accelerated by the warmth of his body beneath the blankets. Thank God you got him here as quickly as you did".

I could not believe my ears.

"Mustard Gas?" I echoed, "God! Will he be all right?"

"It is too early to say," he replied. "There may be some problems with his eyes and the burns on the body are quite severe. Also we don't know how much he has inhaled. We'll do everything possible for him."

I took some deep breaths and composed myself. Then the realisation dawned on me! It was part of army training to place a tiny drop of Mustard Gas liquid on the arm of a soldier so that a decontamination process could be carried out. Somehow the jar of this fearful liquid had been left on open ground.

"Bloody hell, it's still there!" I exclaimed. "Doctor, can you find out exactly where he was at the time of the incident?"

He was able to do so and came back with fairly precise details. By this time an army Captain had arrived and agreed to accompany me to the scene. It was quite a long drive and I drove as fast as I could. By dawn's early light we found the jar fairly easily. It was on its side, bearing no warning marking and still leaking. The grass around it was burned black! I remained there until the officer had arranged for a decontamination squad to make everything safe. In just a few hours time children might have been playing on that open ground!

Shortly after the incident a military Court of Enquiry was held. I was called to give evidence and emphasized that Childs was the victim of an unforeseeable accident which occurred while he was carrying out his duties. No blame was laid at anybody's door and, as far as I am aware, nobody was ever found responsible for the appalling abandonment of such a lethal item.

In the days that followed I made several visits to the hospital and met Mrs Childs who had been notified of her husband's plight. I was relieved that this charming young woman, so recently a bride, would be near to him during what would inevitably be a long period of recovery. I had considerable respect for this quiet and likeable young man, and was distressed by his suffering. In time of war casualties were expected but an accident of this type was so unpredictable (and probably unprecedented) that it was hard to take.

Childs was not returned to his unit and, in the hurly burly of wartime activities I lost touch and never found out what became of him. My unit eventually returned to West London.

24. Missing – Presumed Dead

At about this time I was able to get home on a weekend pass and I took the opportunity to call on Mr and Mrs Mattocks – the parents of my friend Bernard. I rang the doorbell and Mrs Mattocks opened the door. She stepped forward and put her arms around me "Oh Frank, dear boy", she murmured, "I am so pleased to see you". She was trembling and had tears streaming down her face. She led me into the apartment where Mr Mattocks was standing, also visibly distressed.

It was immediately apparent that they had received bad news and in the ensuing moments they explained that they had received a telegram informing them that their son was missing. Apparently his aircraft had failed to return from a bombing mission over Germany.

I was shaken by the news, although I knew (and Bernard knew) that the chances of bomber crews surviving the war were not good. I did my best to keep hope alive. "Perhaps he bailed out and is alive and well. He will turn up sooner or later I am sure". I uttered these words as convincingly as I could but in my heart I knew that the odds were that we would not see Bernard again.

This was a scenario that was being repeated daily all over Britain as relatives received news of the loss of their dear ones, in the case of air crews generally very young men in the prime of their lives. It was always a bitter blow with which it was very hard to come to terms.

As I said goodbye I did my utmost to be as cheerful as possible but I left the apartment with a heavy heart. I knew that

I had lost a very dear friend. No further news of Bernard was ever received.

I kept in touch with his parents and wrote to them regularly, always hoping against hope that good news would be received by them. It was not to be. To lose a beloved son was painful enough – not to have any knowledge of the circumstances in which he died must have made a great loss doubly hard to bear.

25. A Transfer to West Ham

My stay in West London was all too brief and after some reasonably pleasant weeks there I was transferred to an RASC unit in West Ham and housed in a requisitioned block of flats in Manor Road. No pretty girls in this unit and accommodation that was somewhat less comfortable. I was quite pleased, however, to still be within striking distance of my home, with the possibility of an occasional visit.

This particular unit comprised of hundreds of trucks of every kind and, initially, I was in charge of six vehicles but also with a truck of my own.

The work was interesting – there was some long-distance convoy work which took me to various parts of the country, even as far north as Glasgow. As time went by things changed somewhat and our efforts were concentrated on supply work to camps throughout the south east of England and particularly in the area of Wanstead Flats and the London and Tilbury Docks. There was a gradual build-up of facilities and stores and equipment and there was considerable excitement as it became obvious that a lengthy preparation for the assault on Europe was under way.

The day to day running of this unit was controlled by 'Taffy' Davies, a corporal in the transport office. As the demands on the unit intensified the job for this one man became too great, the system buckled and operations became disorganised. My Commanding Officer sent for me.

"I believe you were in an office in Civvy Street," he remarked. "Do you fancy tackling a job in the transport control office?"

I hesitated. I was happy with the job I was doing and the thought of being confined to a dingy office did not appeal to me at all.

The CO sensed my reluctance to volunteer for the job.

"Look here Gianotti," he said, "An army can only function properly if it has a first-class organisation behind every unit. We're in a bloody mess here and I want you to lend a hand to sort things out. The work of this Company is of the utmost importance. I want you to start right away. If the system needs changing – change it! Discuss it all with Corporal Davies, NOW!"

"I understand Sir," I said, "I'll do my very best".

I went immediately to the transport office. 'Taffy' was delighted; he was a friendly man, over 40 years of age, with a weather-beaten grizzly face. He explained how things were done and, having a very orderly mind I quickly perceived that changes were needed and tactfully offered my initial suggestions, cutting out as much of the paperwork as possible to achieve quicker turnaround of vehicles.

Thus started a new phase in my army life. I quickly established a very friendly relationship with 'Taffy'. We worked well together and I applied myself diligently to my new role. The days and weeks passed quickly although I greatly missed the freedom of being on the road. There was little free time – we worked round the clock in shifts but when we could obtain a relief for a few hours we adjourned and proceeded together to the 'Spreadeagle', the local pub, where we enjoyed a few pints of beer with the locals. I was, however, impatient for a change.

After the allied landings in Sicily in July 1943 I had submitted a written request for a transfer to the Italian theatre of war. Was anybody dealing with my application? I discussed the matter with Taffy, explaining that I was eager to be in Italy when the country was finally liberated and when I might be able to trace my family.

"Don't be impatient 'G'", he said. "Nobody will be thinking about your wishes in the present circumstances. You are doing vital work here – relax in that knowledge and think how lucky you are not to be sitting in a slit trench in some muddy field somewhere – with the enemy doing their best to knock hell out of you!"

He was right, of course, I was fully aware of how lucky I had been so far and painfully aware of the suffering and hardships being endured by soldiers, sailors and airmen all over the world. Here at least there were three meals a day and a room in which to sleep. I would have to be patient – it was easier said than done. I had become accustomed to the bombing and the sleepless nights but the frustration and claustrophobic effect of being confined in that control office, when so much was happening all around me, was hard to take.

26. The Liberation of Europe Begins

At the end of May 1944 I was periodically relieved of my control office duties to again take charge of a truck and my journeys took me to some of the 'T' camps spread throughout Southern England.

It was apparent to me that the atmosphere in these camps was very strained – thousands of fighting men trained and ready for action yet confined to their camps under conditions of great secrecy. In the main these troops, knowing that the invasion of Europe was now inevitable, were eager for the offensive to begin. Every day waiting for the action to start was another day of nervousness and growing frustration with fear feeding on delay.

Mercifully, at the beginning of June, heavy troop movements commenced. The roads of Southern England were choked with great convoys carrying troops from many nations. Together with tanks and armoured vehicles they rumbled through the English countryside all going south, and a huge army was assembled at ports all along the Channel coast where a great armada of ships was waiting, ready to leave.

Embarkation started on June 3rd with men being loaded on to ships, ready for departure, but there was further delay due to the bad weather in the Channel. We waited eagerly for news and I felt sorry for the waiting troops, now with their patience almost exhausted. Then, on June 6th, following the despatch of airborne troops late on the previous day, the mighty armada departed and the invasion had begun. The whole operation was carried out under the protection of a gigantic air 'umbrella' and aided by a devastating naval bombardment of the French coast plus massive bombing raids by allied aircraft. By midnight the first 130,000 troops had been landed on the coast of Normandy in the greatest amphibious operation in military history.

Nobody who lived during this momentous time will ever forget the exhilaration, apprehension and fear felt – and the joy of knowing that after nearly five years of war the liberation of the conquered and oppressed peoples of Europe had finally begun.

I marvelled at the incredible feat of planning and organisation that had made this gigantic operation possible and felt privileged that I had been able to play my tiny part.

27. A New Horror – The Flying Bomb

In the middle of June 1944 I had a weekend pass and was able to spend a couple of days at home. By coincidence one of my friends, now a member of the Marine Corps, David Dorgan, was also home on leave and we arranged to visit a local pub together for a quiet lunchtime drink.

As we walked towards our destination – a popular local south London pub – the air raid sirens sounded. We decided to continue and quickened our pace; seconds later we heard a sound we had not previously experienced, it was a combination of the roar of a low-flying aircraft and the spluttering of a motorbike. The sound swiftly increased in intensity and as we looked up to the skies, to our amazement, we saw what looked like an aircraft speeding towards us, emitting a huge flame from its tail end. We hardly had time to draw breath before, suddenly, and when this fearful thing was almost overhead, the engine cut out completely.

David looked at me and I noticed he had gone rather pale.

"Get down Frank", he urged. "It's a f--g bomb!" We dived to the ground to take some cover from a garden wall and waited; there was an uncanny silence which lasted for some seconds and then what seemed like a rustling sound, following by a tremendous explosion. The ground shook beneath us and we remained prostrate on the ground for a moment or two. When we got to our feet we saw a huge pall of smoke rising in a street not too far away. A row of houses had been destroyed. I believe that this was one of the first pilotless flying bombs to be launched at Britain. Rocket-propelled, they travelled at about 350 to 400 mph and carried about 2000 lbs of high explosive. It was a cowardly, most frightening, indiscriminate terror weapon. Thousands were launched at Britain and parts of the Continent, in particular Antwerp in Belgium. Many were shot down by fighter pilots and anti-aircraft guns and some were brought down by barrage balloons but a large proportion got through. Many fell on London where the damage was heavy.

The ramps and launching sites for these weapons, along the French coast, were repeatedly bombed, and we prayed that the invasion of the Continent now proceeding would soon put an end to this new and awful threat.

With their usual ability to humorously make light of almost anything, the British people nicknamed this diabolical weapon the 'Doodlebug!'

On this eventful morning David and I, shaken but undeterred, reached our pub and gratefully consumed a more than welcome pint.

Upon returning from my weekend leave my work at West Ham continued as before.

The allied forces in France had made inroads into enemy territory, sometimes suffering heavy casualties, and the task of supplying our armies was gigantic. My own unit was constantly active and there was little time for any relaxation. I often worked for periods of up to 18 hours at a time in the control office with only short breaks for meals. As a welcome change however I again had some opportunities to drive a truck. On one of these occasions, together with Jimmy Redfern, my co-driver, I was working with a group of vehicles in the dock area of London and once again I was to experience another encounter with a 'Doodlebug'. We were on our way to the docks when the air raid siren sounded; after what seemed like only a few seconds we heard the, by now, familiar roar of an approaching flying bomb. I braked and the truck came to a halt

– there was the usual suspense-filled silence and then a tremendous explosion. This time the bomb had fallen much closer to me than ever before – just a street ahead. The air was filled with flying debris and the sound of glass and roof tiles crashing down. A great column of smoke billowed upwards. We remained still for some seconds to collect our wits, then I started the engine and drove cautiously forward. There was the usual awful scene – houses demolished, some fires burning and dazed people emerging from their shattered homes. Directly opposite us a civilian lorry was leaning at an angle against the side of a half destroyed house. To our amazement the driver was still inside the cab. Although obviously in shock he did not appear to have suffered any physical injury. I realised that his situation was dangerous, pieces of masonry were falling on to the vehicle and he seemed unable to get out. "Hang on," I shouted to him "we'll try to tow you clear". "Jimmy, there's a tow rope in the back – nip out and tie it round our front axle – I'll fix it to the front of the lorry". I drove the truck as close as I could and got out of the cab, grabbing one end of the tow rope I crawled under the front of the lorry and secured it to the front axle. Jimmy fixed his end and I darted back into the cab. I reversed very slowly taking up the slack in the rope. I was perspiring heavily and continued to reverse, not taking my eyes off the lorry as I did so. There was a hideous creaking noise and the lorry surged free, rocking forward on to all four wheels. The debris was still falling from the house. I reversed slowly back for another 10 yards or so, taking both vehicles to a safer position. It had all happened in just a minute or two but it seemed like an eternity! At this moment an ambulance and a fire engine arrived. The ambulance men helped the lorry driver down from his vehicle. Miraculously it seemed that he had sustained no serious injury, but he looked badly shaken.

"Thanks laddie", he said, shaking my hand. "I was bloody scared for a moment".

Jimmy interrupted; "You weren't half as scared as I was", he said, "I thought this mad sod was going to turn you over!"

He was right, of course, I had acted on impulse, judging the situation too perilous to wait for the rescue services to arrive. We had been lucky and now that they were on the spot there was nothing further that we could do, they had to be left to search for dead or wounded citizens, and clear up the devastated area. We went on our way reflecting how wonderfully well all the rescue services coped day after day, night after night. What had been a brief traumatic interlude for us was for them part of their daily routine. The fire brigade, ambulance service, police, air raid wardens – they were all heroes.

28. I Get My Overseas Posting

By July 1944 the allied armies had made great progress. In Italy, where Rome had been taken early in June, the Germans had resisted stubbornly and there were heavy casualties before the Polish army captured the Adriatic port of Ancona on July 15th. In France the allied forces were advancing and the news was also good from the Russian front where the Russian army was on the offensive in all sections. I was by now impatient for overseas service and at the end of the summer I finally had good news. Early one morning Corporal Davies located me at breakfast.

"G," he said, "Your posting has arrived. You'll get some embarkation leave and then report to a holding company in Leeds".

"Where am I bound for?" I asked, somewhat naively.

"You know I don't know that," he replied, "but I hope you get your wish and get to Italy". Then, after a pause, "We are both off duty this evening, come and have a few beers with me at the 'Spreadeagle'". That evening, as we enjoyed our drinks together, Taffy made no bones about how he felt about my departure. "You're a daft bugger. A posting overseas means you'll lose your stripe and you'll be sticking your neck out when you might easily have spent the rest of the war in England".

I appreciated his sentiments but promotion in the army was not something about which I was enthusiastic and I hungered for a change of scene. In any event the die was cast.

The evening passed pleasantly and Taffy became quite sentimental, in an almost paternal manner. Looking at me closely through bleary eyes he said, "G", I'm going to miss you very much, you've done a great job here, much more important than you could have imagined." Then, leaning forward, he tapped the side of his nose as one does when about to reveal a secret. "Your performance with this company has not gone unnoticed by the people at HQ. I can't say more but, take my word for it, you'll hear more in due course". I smiled and, feeling sure that it was the beer talking, promptly dismissed the matter from my mind.

A few days later my embarkation leave started and I enjoyed a welcome rest at home. I felt quite excited at the prospect of an overseas posting but my mother did not share my enthusiasm.

"Don't worry," I assured her, "the worst of the war is now over and I'll soon be back home for good."

After my period of leave I reported to a holding company in Leeds where I was to await further instructions. My stay in Leeds was brief – just a few days. Then, with a group of other soldiers, I was moved up to Glasgow where large numbers of men were being assembled in camps near the port. Here we were issued with khaki drill uniform – usually issued to men serving in the Far East – and I was depressed at the possibility of being sent to the Japanese theatre of war. I was cheered up, however, by one of the group who pointed out that at this time of year KD would also be worn in North Africa and Italy.

Again my stay was brief but I had the chance to get into town on a couple of evenings and enjoy the company of the local people who were most kind and eager to show the troops true Scottish hospitality.

Swiftly we were informed that embarkation was now imminent and we were transported to the docks and taken on board what I think was an American 'Liberty Ship'. I could not believe my luck. The ship was bright and clean and food was served in quite pleasant dining areas on large trays, quite a treat after tin plates or mess-tins! Alas, only one night was spent on that vessel; after a few hours we were awakened by an alarm and by shouted instructions from the ship's crew. "Everybody on deck – move quickly – the ship's on fire!" There was no evidence of any flames or smoke and with no panic the ship was quickly evacuated. My recollections of that night are hazy except for the memory of the swearing and cursing of hundreds of bleary-eyed men. There was no explanation of exactly where the fire had taken place, although there were some vague rumours of an attempt to sabotage the ship. It was of no further consequence – after a few hours of confusion we were transferred to another vessel, this time a Norwegian troopship. This was not nearly as pleasant – troops were packed into crowded quarters and the hammocks in which we would sleep were so close together that only if you possessed considerable gymnastic skills was it possible to get in and out without crashing into the hammocks all around you. The first night aboard was miserable. Even though the ship was in port the movement in the water and the unfamiliar hammock, plus the foul atmosphere below deck, made things very uncomfortable. It was evident that our voyage would be no luxury cruise!

29. Destination Unknown

I awoke early the following morning and, after a wash and shave in cramped conditions, joined the assembled troops on deck. It was a great relief to feel the wind on my face and I breathed deeply, filling my lungs with the clean salt air. Our ship was one of dozens forming a huge convoy, to be escorted by destroyers and other naval vessels.

The convoy left without delay and I thrilled at the breathtaking sight of so many ships together and wondered at the feat of organisation that made everything happen with such precision. The sailors on board were splendid, cheerful men, helpful in every way but they could give no indication of where our destination could be. Time passed very quickly on board, the hours being punctuated by physical training on deck, some weapons training, and breaks for meals.

As we moved into the Atlantic the sea became rough and a good many soldiers suffered seasickness. I was lucky in not suffering in this respect and indeed, having a healthy appetite, enjoyed disposing of some of the unconsumed rations of my unfortunate friends. Eventually the convoy traversed the Bay of Biscay and passed through the Straits of Gibraltar by night, entering the Mediterranean Sea. The following morning the weather was much improved with a calm sea and a beautiful clear blue sky. The convoy was sailing close to the coast of North Africa which was observed with great interest from the deck.

During this voyage, apart from some submarine alerts which may well have been routine practice operations, there was no evidence of any enemy activity. I recalled the vicious air attacks previously made on our convoys passing through the Mediterranean, and the heavy losses of men and ships, and was thankful that I had not had to make the same voyage earlier in the war when our command of sea and sky had not been so complete.

It was not long before I had my first clear indication that we were probably bound for Italy and I became excited at the prospect. Sections of the convoy, including our ship, started to peel off northwards, passing Sicily on the right. There was now a murmur from the troops on board, "It's Naples! We're bound for Naples!"

30. I Set Foot on Italian Soil

As we approached the Italian coastline my feeling of excitement at the prospect of landing in this theatre of war was tempered by thoughts and worries about my mother, alone at home. In early September the Germans had introduced a new terror weapon, the 'V2', a huge rocket packed with explosives. These were being launched indiscriminately against British cities. They could not be intercepted and arrived without warning, causing heavy damage and loss of life. Despite massive allied air attacks on the launching sites in Europe these attacks were continuing. My thoughts were interrupted as Naples came into sight, with a view of the port, in its huge bay, and the sight of the towering mass of Mount Vesuvius.

Disembarkation proceeded very rapidly and I finally set foot on Italian soil. I was astonished to see the vast extent of the damage inflicted on the port by the allied bombing and shelling and the incredible amount of activity; men, supplies, armoured vehicles being landed from ships constantly disgorging all the paraphernalia of war.

During the inevitable waiting about while troops were being assembled for despatch to their various destinations I had time to think again about my mother. I prayed that she was well and reflected on how excited she would be if she could know that I had arrived in my father's homeland.

I listened to the babble of voices from the Italian civilians working in the port and was painfully aware of the fact that I knew nothing of the language. I caught the eye of one Italian working on the quayside.

"Buon giorno" he said, politely.

"Buon giorno", I replied, reproducing his pronunciation as accurately as I could. I had uttered my first words in Italian and felt quite exhilarated. I did not know what the future would have in store for me but at that moment I vowed that, as soon as I was adjusted to my new environment, I would start to learn the language. I would mix with Italians whenever I could and obtain books on Italian so that I could learn as much as possible as quickly as possible and when, God willing, the army liberated the North of Italy I would endeavour to locate my Italian family.

From the port of Naples, with a group of other soldiers, I was transported by a troop-carrying vehicle to the little Southern Italian town of Nola, to the east of the port. Here we were accommodated for just a few days in a very large barracks prior to being posted to a regular unit. The quarters were reasonably comfortable and the food quite good.

We were kept busy with the routine training and spent a fair amount of time drilling on the massive barrack square. The days were still very hot and I welcomed the cool of the evenings when there were opportunities to enjoy a drink or two with the lads with whom I became friendly, in the various bars in the town. Nola was not as I had imagined an Italian town would be like. I could not believe the squalor and the poverty that existed. As we walked through the narrow streets we were regularly approached by local villains and even children, some very young, offering to buy our rations of cigarettes, soap, etc or alternatively offering the services of the town's prostitutes, describing their physical attributes and services offered in quaint but very descriptive broken English – leaving little to the imagination! In general, however, I found the Italian people to be cheerful, friendly and helpful.

There was just one opportunity to visit Naples. With two friends I travelled by train, having obtained a day pass. I was fascinated by the poorer section ('off limits' to allied troops). I wanted to see much more but time had flown and we only just caught the last train back to Nola. In the morning it was announced that a posting had been arranged.

With a large group I travelled eastwards across Italy by train to the port of Bari. We travelled by night and I recall vividly one particular event. Part way across the country the train halted at a small Italian town (I believe it was Benevento) and we descended from our railway carriage for a 'feeding halt'. By now the weather had changed dramatically; it was raining heavily and conditions were cold and miserable. The food, a meat and vegetable stew, served from hot steaming tubs, was scooped into our mess tins under a crudely erected shelter by the side of the track. The shelter had open ends and the wind blew in driving rain as we stood while we ate. At the end of the shelter from which we were to make our exit there was a large oil drum in which we could empty any food remaining in our mess tins. By the side of the drum there were four small children, one only about five years of age. They wore tattered clothes and looked pale and cold. They were waiting to gratefully intercept any slops, which they accepted in open tins and devoured instantly. I was deeply touched and gave them some bread that I still held and a small piece of chocolate that I had kept for the journey. The duty Sergeant noticed. "Watch yourself lad", he grunted, "these little sods are desperate – they'll nick anything, even the watch off your wrist if you give them half a chance". I nodded, to indicate that I had got the message but inwardly I felt great sympathy for these little waifs – it would take a very hard man not to feel compassion for these children of war. This was my first experience of this kind but it was not unique in this war torn land. I was to witness many similar scenes in my travels in the ensuing months and years. We boarded the train again and resumed our journey but it moved very slowly, stopping regularly for reasons unknown. When we reached Bari we had a period of waiting, assembled outside the railway station, and were then taken to the port where we boarded a ship. We were informed that our destination was Ancona, the Adriatic port to the North.

The ship sailed without too much delay but was packed with troops and this, combined with a choppy sea and a feeling of extreme weariness, made for an uncomfortable voyage. I managed to find a place below deck where I could rest against my pack and kitbag and snatched a few hours of fitful sleep.

31. I Join My New Company

Soon after we disembarked from our ship I was transported, with my group, to our new unit (a General Transport Company of the RASC) based in the centre of Ancona. I felt rather exhausted and was relieved to know that I would now probably have a regular base. I had been moving from place to place since leaving my unit at West Ham and disliked the constant disruption. However, I knew that moving frequently was inevitable in a soldier's life and was becoming accustomed to this nomadic existence, carrying all my possessions in a backpack and kit bag and constantly saying goodbye to friends made along the way. Now perhaps I would be settled with new comrades for a while. The company was accommodated in a number of fairly large buildings, with vehicles of every kind located in streets and squares in the immediate vicinity. Conditions were good, by Army standards, and the sleeping arrangements (wooden beds with the usual palliasse and blankets) were as expected.

I learned that the company was mainly engaged in moving supplies of every kind to wherever needed.

The Italian campaign had been long and hard with the Germans fighting bitter defensive battles and contesting every inch of ground, with mountains and rivers presenting great problems to the allied forces. The forward troops were some miles to the North making slow progress not helped, I gathered, by the withdrawal of large numbers of troops to the western front.

The fact that the allies now had such air superiority provided a feeling of relative security and it was difficult to appreciate that not many miles away men were dying daily in bloody combat in awful conditions. I was swiftly allocated a 3-ton truck and my first weeks were spent on night driving, mainly moving supplies from the port of Ancona to ammunition dumps and supply depots further north. We drove using sidelights, the nights were long and the conditions cold and wet.

I soon adjusted to sleeping during the day and during off-duty periods, before resuming the nightly routine, I had time to make the acquaintance of new friends, two of these being Sid Riley from Sutton Coldfield and Arthur Watcham from London, both lively and likeable young men of my own age. We spent a good deal of time together and got to know Ancona quite well. I discovered, to my delight, that there was a YMCA building in the centre of the town where it was possible to study the Italian language and I seized the opportunity to attend whenever I could. I was thus able to obtain at least some knowledge of the verbs and acquired a basic vocabulary. During periods at night when waiting for my vehicle to be loaded or unloaded I frequently found Italians with whom I could converse. Initially I found this difficult but gradually I improved. I gathered that my pronunciation was good but found the Italian grammar difficult to grasp. I was not too concerned; I would persevere so that I would be reasonably well prepared should I ultimately be able to locate my Italian family.

The last weeks of 1944 passed very slowly and I longed for the spring and the better weather that spring would bring. I felt somewhat frustrated that progress by the advance troops was slow and I eagerly awaited the time when we could move North.

For the moment, however, I knew that patience was required. Not every soldier could be with the forward troops and I was aware that for every infantryman there had to be many more troops engaged in the business of providing the materials of war to the men doing the fighting. The monotony of the nightly ferrying of supplies was broken by some convoy work in daytime. Being on the road with my friends was a pleasant relief and I became very well acquainted with towns and villages throughout the 'Marches' – the Adriatic province of Italy. The movement of troops to and from the front was constant and consisted of men from all over the world – Americans, Australians, New Zealanders, Poles, Indians, South Africans and others. Mixing with men from so many countries was fascinating. I was intrigued to find that many of the Polish troops had a good knowledge of the Italian language and I had frequent opportunities to enjoy conversations in Italian with those Poles who were not so fluent in English. It all seemed a million miles away from home!

32. Honoured by King and Country

On a day in early January 1945 I was awakened from my slumbers in the late afternoon by my good friend Sid Riley. I knew I was due for a driving detail that night but had not expected to be disturbed so soon.

"What's up Sid?" I asked, somewhat irritably.

"Nothing much G," he replied "except that I thought you should know before you leave that your name is on the Company Orders noticeboard – you are due before the CO at 9.30 in the morning. What have you been up to?"

I couldn't begin to imagine. I cast my mind back to try to recall any detectable offence I might have committed in recent days but nothing sprang to mind. Being unable to gather any information from anybody I ate my dinner and set off in my truck. The weather was now very bad and as I eased my vehicle through the swirling mists along the Adriatic coast, to and from the port and supply depots further to the North, I sought a reason for my morning appointment. Could there be bad news from England regarding my mother or brothers? I didn't think so as any such news would have been conveyed to me immediately. Perhaps I might be promoted again? I didn't particularly want promotion; being a driver with only the responsibility of one's vehicle and the relative freedom enjoyed when on the road was, to me, not only a useful wartime function but one of the more satisfactory ways of enduring the military life.

"Forget it Frank," I muttered to myself, "all will be revealed in the morning".

At 9.25 am, after a wash and shave and some breakfast, I presented myself, in best battledress and shiny boots, at the CO's office. In accordance with the usual procedure, I was marched in by the Sergeant Major. My cap was not removed, indicating that I was not 'on a charge' which was a relief. As I entered, the CO and another officer both stood up and, to my astonishment, greeted me with broad smiles. The CO extended his hand and shook mine warmly.

"What feats did you perform in England, Gianotti?" he enquired.

I was taken aback, "I really don't know Sir," I replied, "what do you mean?"

"What I mean," he said, "is that you must have done something rather special. It is my great pleasure to inform you that your name appeared in the New Year's Honours List. You have been awarded the British Empire Medal."

I could hardly believe my ears! In the ensuing moments there was a brief pleasant conversation in which I answered questions about my army service in England, and then the CO congratulated me again.

"We are glad to have you in this Company, Gianotti, now get down to QM stores, draw your medal ribbon and sew it onto your battledress. Wear it with pride."

"Thank you Sir," I replied, "I feel very honoured".

It was only as I left the office that the words of Corporal Davies when we enjoyed our last drink together, the words I had dismissed so lightly, came flooding back into my mind.

"...take my word for it, you'll hear more in due course."

The old devil had known about a recommendation but had divulged nothing of it to me.

I had never been too concerned about awards or medals. I always felt that too many brave men, killed or wounded in battle, received nothing. I was, nevertheless, pleased. In particular I savoured the irony of the fact that I, the son of an Italian and barred from working for any Government organisation in peacetime (even the Post Office!) had, in war, been honoured by King and Country.

When I emerged from the CO's office my good friends Riley and Watcham were quickly on the scene – eager to know what had happened.

"What have you been copped for?" said Sid, wickedly. "How much jankers have you got?"

I delayed replying, deliberately, so that my words would have maximum impact.

"No, actually, I have been awarded a medal," I replied, "a British Empire Medal."

They both looked at me incredulously for a moment or two.

"You lying bastard," said Watcham.

"Come on 'G', tell us the truth."

When I had explained and convinced them that I was not pulling their legs they were both delighted and shook my hand warmly.

"The Great 'G' a bloody hero eh!" uttered Sid.

They both stood to attention, saluted and salaamed in mock obeisance.

That evening, with one or two others, we celebrated in a little local bar, returning to our quarters all feeling very merry, if a little the worse for wear, by the obligatory hour of 23.59.

It had been a memorable day in my life.

33. Victory In Sight (and I Meet Maria)

The following months passed slowly. Day after day, night after night, the routine continued. We transported so much ammunition, bombs, and supplies of every kind that I wondered at times if my company alone was supplying the whole army and air force! In my travels I was often in small towns or villages and I could observe how devastating the war had been. There was much poverty but despite this I always found the Italian people to be friendly and generous with what little they had to offer. Quite often when on long distance details and driving in convoys I would halt with my friends at locations we came to know and exchange our tins of 'M & V' and other army rations for fresh bread, hunks of cheese and bottles of red wine. I enjoyed these occasions greatly and as my Italian was now improving I was able to interpret for the other lads. I was beginning to know a little more about Italy and felt a great affection for the Italian people. As a break from routine there would be an occasional free day. On one of these, and desiring a change from the company of my friends, I took a long walk in Ancona, along the cliff path overlooking the sea. It was a bright sunny day, although still quite cold, and I felt very relaxed as I gazed at the beautiful Adriatic Sea. During my walk I observed a very pretty Italian girl in peasant-style dress sitting on a wooden seat. It was very difficult to make any contact with respectable Italian girls but I decided to try. I said "Buon giorno, signorina" and, in my very best Italian asked if I might talk to her for a few moments while I rested. Initially a little frightened and obviously very shy she became more comfortable once she knew that I had some knowledge of the language. She was small, dark and had most beautiful brown eyes and in no time at all I discovered that her name was Maria, she was eighteen years of age, the daughter of a local barber and lived with her parents in a cottage further along the cliff. I told her a little about myself and of my Italian origin, and my desire to eventually locate my Italian relatives. She was very intrigued. She had been on an errand and had to return home but before she left I asked if I might meet her again. After a moment of hesitation she pointed out her cottage and said that I might call if passing at any time. I shook her hand and thanked her. I was reluctant to let go!

Free days such as these were few and far between but I had this girl on my mind, remembering her kind and gentle manner and bewitching smile. I was determined to see her again and when my next free day came along I called at her home. She was there together with her father and mother and I was invited in and offered a glass of wine. They were obviously simple Italian folk and once I had broken the ice seemed to take kindly to me. I had taken some chocolate and cigarettes as a gift for them and these were gratefully accepted. After this first call I saw Maria on several occasions and became very fond of her. Generally her parents would be present or in close attendance and the opportunities to be alone together were rare and precious. The war was still raging and my army duties very demanding, also I was aware that my stay in Ancona would be short and my future afterwards could not be predicted. All the circumstances made the prospect of any serious romantic involvement remote, and we both knew it. Our short friendship had been beautiful. On our last date I kissed her goodbye and felt infinitely sad. It was unlikely that we would meet again but I was grateful for the time we had spent together.

The progress of the war in Italy was now fast gaining momentum and there were all the signs of a build-up for one final offensive. It could not be long now – at last final victory was in sight.

34. The End of the War in Italy

In mid April 1945 we received news of great successes by the allied forces in Northern Italy. Earlier in the month, after months of stalemate, a huge offensive had been launched – supported by massive numbers of bombers and fighter bombers. Bologna was captured and the whole of the German resistance was rapidly collapsing. Then, on April 25th, a great uprising of Italian partisans started and on April 28th the Italian dictator Benito Mussolini and his mistress Clara Petacci who had been captured by them were shot. Their bodies were transported to Milan where they were hung upside down on public display – a terrible but fitting end for the pompous, vain, would-be Caesar who had dragged the Italian people into a disastrous war. On April 30th 1945 the news I had been waiting and praying for came through – Turin and Milan had been occupied by the allies! On May 2nd at noon, as the result of a surrender document signed by German envoys three days earlier, the war in Italy came to an end.

There was great rejoicing by everybody in the Company. Now, at last, with the allied armies in Germany in the last stages of a long and bloody campaign and the Russians fighting bitter battles in the streets of Berlin, surely the war in Europe must be nearly over.

Amid all the rejoicing I felt apprehensive about the welfare of my Italian relatives. Enquiries I had made months earlier through the Red Cross had not met with any response. There was little I could do at that moment but I was determined to make every effort to locate them as soon as possible. I contemplated asking for a special leave but decided to wait until the dust had settled; my knowledge of the language was slowly improving and I was now able to converse reasonably well so long as conversations were confined to every-day simple subjects. I would persevere so that I would be able to cope if and when the opportunity came.

35. The End of the War in Germany

On May 7th 1945 the unconditional surrender of all German forces was signed at the Headquarters of General Eisenhower at Rheims, following the announcement the previous week that Adolph Hitler and his mistress Eva Braun had committed suicide on April 30th in their Berlin bunker.

On May 8th 1945 the Germans surrendered to the USSR. The great joy of victory was tempered by news of the awful suffering that had been endured by all the nations that had been the victims of German conquest, and in particular the occupants of the Nazi concentration camps. Earlier in the war I had nursed some doubts as to the truth of all the reports of atrocities being committed and thought these might have been exaggerated for propaganda purposes. Now, with the liberation of the death camps, the awful truth was revealed and the scale of the torture and mass extermination of human beings filled me with horror. Thank God it was all over. The war had lasted nearly six years. Now I had the distant prospect of returning home to civilian life but the demobilisation process, on a numbered 'first-in first-out' basis, would be slow and I did not contemplate being released for 18 months or so. My army days were far from over.

36. I Find My Uncle Giovanni

In June 1945 I decided that it was the right time to ask for leave, with a view to locating my family in the North of Italy.

My enquiries through the Red Cross had not been acknowledged and I had no news at all regarding the welfare of my relatives, in fact I did not even know if they were alive.

I arranged an interview with my Commanding Officer to request leave and explained to him that I was in possession of some old addresses of a number of uncles, aunts and cousins in Milan, Turin and Ivrea. I stressed how anxious I was to have news of them all and, indeed, to finally get to know them.

He was very understanding, and co-operative.

"Right Gianotti," he said, "You can have 14 days leave. I can't help you with transport so you'll have to make your own way up there. I will give you a special letter, addressed to all Allied Commands, detailing the reason for your leave and requesting that they should assist you in any way possible". He continued, "You have not done too badly in your Army service so far- you deserve this break. You can go the day after tomorrow. I wish you every success". He smiled and added, wagging his finger, "Make sure you get back in 14 days or I'll have you crucified!"

I was very grateful for this great opportunity and somewhat excited by the challenge it presented.

The next 48 hours passed very slowly. Although the distances I proposed to travel were not great by today's standards I knew that 'hitch-hiking' in the conditions then existing would not be easy. On the morning of my departure from Ancona, therefore, I got up very early, shaved, had a good breakfast and scrounged some sandwiches from the cookhouse which I hoped would see me through the day. The weather was fine and very warm and I knew that I would find the going easier if I travelled light. I was dressed in my KD uniform, wearing boots. In my backpack I took only a pair of shoes, a spare shirt and a change of underclothes and socks, plus my shaving kit, my camera and all the money I had been able to save, plus a blanket-roll in case I had to 'sleep rough'.

I had been advised that there were some trains running from Ancona to Bologna and I decided to start this part of my journey by train. My great friend Sid Riley accompanied me to the railway station. "There's a bevy for you 'G'," he said, handing me a bottle of red wine, "The best of luck – and be bloody careful, I don't want to lose my interpreter!" He gave my arm a friendly squeeze and left me to wait for a train. This arrived after about half an hour. It was a very old and dirty goods train, packed with Indian troops being transported north.

I climbed into an open wagon in which there were about 20 Indian soldiers. Two of them pulled me aboard – fine-looking men with their turbans and uniforms, looking very smart and clean despite the rough travelling conditions. I settled down into a corner making myself as comfortable as possible against the side of the wagon.

There was some delay in starting and then the train departed, making very slow progress along the Adriatic Coast. One of the Indians offered me some tea, brewed on a portable stove. "Char Johnny?", he enquired, "Very hot and very sweet". I accepted gratefully. There was very little subsequent conversation and after enjoying views of the beautiful Adriatic Sea as we passed through Senigallia and Pesaro I dozed off. When I awoke after what seemed a long time I observed that we had halted. We had only reached Rimini. There was a long delay here and I took the opportunity to leave the wagon and stretch my legs. The whole area around Rimini had been badly hit by the fighting and had been heavily bombed. I gazed at the devastation and wondered how long it would be before this would once again be a holiday resort for tourists. I sat down on a grassy bank beside the train and ate my sandwiches, helped down by swigs of wine from Riley's bottle which induced a feeling of relaxation. Eventually there was considerable activity further up the line and I clambered aboard as the train began to move. The train left the sea at Rimini and the rest of the journey was uneventful. There were several more halts before we finally arrived in Bologna in the late afternoon. I decided that I would not travel any further that day. After making enquiries and covering a few miles on foot I located an Army transit camp in the centre of town. I presented my letter and was told that I could sleep the night there. I had no great desire to partake of any army food and, leaving my pack etc behind, I explored the historic town of Bologna. Eventually, feeling tired and hungry I went into a small trattoria and ordered a meal. The food was magnificent and the wine superb and it was all quite inexpensive.

I got into conversation with an Italian family dining there – a father and mother with adult son and daughter. They were intrigued to hear of my mission and were most generous with their hospitality. We drank a fair quantity of wine before I left, with their good wishes, and it was nearly midnight before I reached the Camp. I slept very well that night!

The following morning I was awake before 6 am. I had a shave and a shower and ate a good breakfast. I was again able to obtain some sandwiches from the cookhouse. I was anxious to make better progress than the day before. The orderly Sergeant was very helpful. "I've got a truck going to Modena at 8 o'clock" he said, "if you look sharp you can have a lift". I was directed to the vehicle – an open 15-cwt truck. The driver and another soldier sat in the cab and I made myself as comfortable as possible in the back of the vehicle.

This part of the journey was very interesting. Again I was able to observe how much damage the war had caused. I had time to reflect on the change in the architecture and the general appearance of the Italian people, compared with the poverty and squalor of the south. We stopped only once and the driver gave me some tea from a flask. Upon arrival in Modena we passed through the centre of the town. I was impressed by the great avenues, spacious squares and the beautiful cathedral. Eventually the truck stopped. The driver got out "Here we are pal," he said, "I've brought you to the main road for Milan. Good luck on the rest of your journey". I thanked him for his help and walked to a junction where vehicles would have to slow down.

I had lettered the words 'MILAN PLEASE' on a large piece of white cardboard and I held this up to every passing vehicle. It was not long before I had some luck. A staff car stopped, driven by a British soldier. "Can't do Milan," he said. "How will Piacenza do? It's as far as I am going". "Wonderful" I replied. Piacenza was directly on my route, and within striking distance of Milan.

The car sped off and I sank into the unaccustomed luxury of the cushioned seat. The driver was in a hurry and travelled at high speed whenever the road was clear enough. We had a pleasant conversation and the time passed quickly. We passed through many interesting and colourful villages and I had a passing glimpse of Parma. In no time, it seemed, we arrived in Piacenza. I was taken to a suitable point from which I hoped I would be able to reach Milan fairly easily. I waited by the roadside for a short while and was ignored by a number of vehicles, civilian and military. Eventually an army truck stopped. It was an open 15-cwt and, again, the driver had a passenger in front. "Jump aboard" the driver shouted, "I can take you almost to the centre of Milan". This time the ride was not going to be so comfortable. The truck was laden with boxes of supplies. I moved these about to give myself a makeshift seat using my blanket to make a back cushion. I ate my sandwiches which were not very appetising and were in stark contrast to the banquet I had enjoyed the night before. I was covered in white dust from the roads. It was, by now, very hot and I began to feel stiff and tired. Fortunately this part of the journey was relatively short. In due course we arrived in Milan and I was dropped about a mile from the cathedral. There was a small café nearby and I seized the opportunity to freshen myself up and to enjoy several cups of coffee.

I took out my list of addresses. My first point of call was to be the VIALE MONTE NERO where one of my father's brothers, Giovanni, was listed as living at number 34. The café owner gave me instructions on how to reach my destination. I took a tram which passed quite close to the beautiful cathedral. It was a relatively short journey and when I left the tram I soon found the address I required. It was in a pleasant residential section of the town. The number 34 covered a small block of apartments. I began to feel a growing sense of excitement. Was my uncle still alive? Did he still live at this address? How would I be received? I was, after all, a soldier in what had been an enemy army. I hoped that blood would prove to be thicker than water!

I went into the entrance of the apartment block. Inside was a cabinet containing a list of names. Alongside each name was a push button. Below was a grille into which I assumed one could speak. My eyes ran swiftly down the list. There it was – G

GIANOTTI. My heart missed a beat! My knowledge of the Italian language was still far from perfect and I opted to avoid the problems that might result from the use of the bell and speaker. There was a young woman cleaning the floors. I asked her on which floor Signor Gianotti could be found. "Secondo Piano" she said, abruptly. I made my way up to the second floor and found my uncle's name on a door. I pressed the bell and waited for what seemed an eternity. Eventually, after much rattling of bolts, the door opened, still partially secured by a door chain. A woman's face peered out. She looked apprehensive. I had no idea who she was.

"Cosa vuole?" she enquired.

"Buon giorno, Signora" I replied,

"Cerco Signor Gianotti, sono suo nipote Inglese". She was clearly taken aback and temporarily speechless.

"Si Signora", I said, reassuringly, "Mi chiamo Gianotti".

The next few minutes were sheer delight – almost like something from a Whitehall farce – she threw open the door and embraced me. It was obvious that she could see that I was tired and travel weary and she hurried to prepare a bath for me, at the same time explaining that she was Signora Molteni, a widow and the sister-in-law of Giovanni, whose wife had died five or six years earlier. She was a small elderly woman, lean and with grey hair. She ran everywhere at high speed! She lived in a section of the apartment with her only son Ottavio. Due to her highly excitable state I hardly had time to collect my wits before she had removed my jacket and steered me into the bathroom, urging me to get in and to leave the door unlocked. I complied, sinking my weary limbs into the splendidly hot bath water. Within seconds she re-appeared, placing a jug of red wine on the stool beside the bath. "Beve! Beve!" she urged. I did not need telling twice – my throat was parched, and the wine cool and delicious. After a minute or two of calm she charged in again, this time with her coat on, explaining that she was off to inform my uncle of my arrival. Apparently his place of work was quite nearby and although it was near the end of his working day she could not wait to give him the news. She scurried off and, resisting the temptation to laze in the bath, I quickly dried myself, dressed, and went into a small but comfortable lounge taking my wine with me. I sank into an armchair . "Is this all a dream?" I asked myself. My thoughts were swiftly interrupted, Signora Molteni had returned with my uncle. Giovanni came through the door and embraced me warmly, kissing me on both cheeks. We stood back and looked at each other. He bore a very strong resemblance to my father, a small lightly built man, in his late sixties, almost bald and with a high intelligent forehead and the most beautiful clear blue eyes that twinkled as he spoke. He was eager to know how I had fared during my wartime experiences in Italy and, in particular, to have news of my mother and brothers. I explained that they were all well when I last had a letter from home. We talked briefly of my father and about his death and his eyes filled with tears. They had been very close in their youth. He was altogether a most kind and loveable man and I immediately felt great affection for him. Shortly afterwards Ottavio arrived.

Ottavio was tall, sun-tanned and handsome. He had a moustache which turned upwards at the ends, giving him an amiable and somewhat cavalier appearance. He was unmarried and I imagined that he would be very attractive to women. My uncle, having ascertained what time I had available, and not wishing to lose time from his work, said that he would place me in the care of his nephew for a couple of days.

Ottavio was free and readily agreed to conduct me on a tour of Milan. He also insisted on vacating his bed for me and I had a wonderful night's sleep between sheets – the first time I had enjoyed this luxury for many months.

37. I Sample 'La Dolce Vita'

The following morning we got up early and after a light continental breakfast set off. Walking and using trams we visited the magnificent cathedral, saw the Scala Opera House, various museums and some pleasant parks and gardens, our tour interrupted only by what Ottavio said would be a short break for lunch at a small restaurant. We were there for almost two hours! It was very enjoyable. That evening Ottavio took me to visit a close friend of his – Signor Constantino Pallavidini. This gentleman was a wealthy Italian fruit merchant and lived in a sumptuous apartment in an exclusive part of town. He was a very elegant and sophisticated man, probably in his mid-thirties. He greeted us warmly, then explained that he was giving a party at his apartment that evening. He invited us to attend. Ottavio accepted immediately.

We adjourned to a nearby bar for a glass or two of Campari Soda and returned to the apartment at about 9 o'clock. What I saw when I entered the apartment was totally unexpected. The floors were of marble, highly polished, and the rooms furnished with beautiful antique furniture and exquisite curtains – the whole place was luxurious to a degree that I could not have imagined. Constantino introduced me to his friends, some handsome young men and three or four very beautiful women, all exquisitely dressed. They each kissed me on both cheeks. I felt very elated but was painfully aware of how out of place I must have seemed in my army clothes. I was thankful that I was, at least, wearing a pair of clean and shiny shoes!

There was a great deal of food and drink provided and time passed very pleasantly. For a while I became the centre of attraction and was bombarded with questions about life in England in wartime, my time in Italy etc. To converse in Italian with a group, all speaking at high speed, was a strain. The pressure was eased when Ottavio appeared with some recording equipment. He thrust a microphone under my nose! "Franco, record a message for your mother", he said. By this time I found it difficult to think in English but I managed a garbled message. (I subsequently received the record that was produced. I did, in fact, post it home to my mother and it is still in my possession).

The party by now was becoming quite merry. There was some dancing to lively Italian records and there was a marvellous party atmosphere. The alcohol consumed during the day was having its effect and I felt as if I was walking on air. I noticed that Ottavio was staggering about, obviously rather drunk. I steeled myself. One of us had to stay in control. The fun continued until about 2 am. Ottavio disappeared, accompanied by one of the girls. Gradually each of the guests departed. Each one embraced me warmly before leaving. Constantino suggested that it would probably be a good idea if I stayed the night. He had a comfortable settee in the lounge and provided a sheet and a blanket. Having ascertained that I was comfortable he went off to his room. Before he left I asked if Ottavio was OK. "Si Franco," he said "Ottavio é molto felice". I had been more concerned with Ottavio's health than his happiness but my smile of acknowledgement indicated that I had got the message! I turned out the light. The air was heavy with the aroma of perfume. I was asleep before my head touched the pillow!

It was mid-morning before I was awakened by an elderly woman who turned out to be Constantino's housemaid. She brought me some coffee which was more than welcome, easing my parched throat and bringing me back to life. I dressed and, just as I had finished, Ottavio poked his head around the door. He looked dreadful but managed a grin. "Andiamo, Franco," he croaked. I said goodbye to Constantino, thanking him profusely for what had been a most splendid and dreamlike evening. He told me that he proposed to visit England in the not too distant future, on matters concerning fruit exports, and he asked me to write to him when I was finally demobilised. (Several years were to pass before I eventually met him in London).

Leaving Constantino we travelled back to the Viale Monte Nero by tram. We were greeted at the apartment by Signora Molteni. She was none too pleased with her son for keeping me out all night. "Imbecile! Delinquente! Birbante!" she shrieked, hurling these and other choice epithets at her bleary-eyed son. The onslaught ceased when I explained that I had enjoyed myself immensely. Ottavio retired to bed and I had a pleasant day strolling around the streets of Milan and spending some more time in the magnificent cathedral. In the late afternoon I returned, stopping at a small café on the corner of the Viale Monte Mero which Ottavio had indicated to me the day before. This was run by two charming sisters, very sweet young girls, with whom I enjoyed a most pleasant conversation and a glass of wine before returning to the apartment. That evening we had an excellent dinner consisting of typical Italian dishes, helped down with some superb local wine. Afterwards the four of us enjoyed an hour or so of relaxed conversation.

It was obvious to me that my uncle was a man of modest means and I was quite touched by the lengths to which he and the others had gone to entertain me.

The following day would be Saturday leaving my uncle free. "Domani," he announced, "Andiamo a Torino". I knew that the main body of my Italian family lived in Turin and I was thrilled by the prospect of meeting them.

38. The Family Greet Me in Turin

Early on Saturday morning I walked with my uncle Giovanni to the railway station in Milan where we boarded the train for Turin. The journey was uneventful and we chatted together for a while before he dozed off. I was still recovering from the excesses of the previous two days. The party had been a most extraordinary event, totally unexpected in a country that had been so devastated by the war. I knew that Signor Pallavidini's lifestyle was by no means typical of the average family life at this time and I was eagerly awaiting my meeting with my relatives in Turin.

I gazed out of the carriage window taking in the local countryside – mile after mile of flat country with workers toiling in the rice fields – and I thought of my mother, alone at home, and how she would have loved to be with me.

The train was not fast and we stopped at a number of stations. Upon arrival in Turin my uncle informed me that our first call would be at the shop owned by my cousin, Gina. It was just a short tram ride from the station. During the journey I was able to see a little of the beautiful city of Turin with its streets set out in straight lines and its characteristic style of buildings so different from those in the streets of Milan. We arrived at our destination in the centre of Turin, an attractive little bakery with assorted cakes displayed in the windows and emitting the wonderful aroma of freshly baked bread.

Gina was at the door and Giovanni introduced us. She was about 10 years my senior, short and dark-haired and obviously very excitable. She threw her arms around me and kissed me affectionately on both cheeks, tears of joy streaming down her face, then led me inside to meet her husband Mario, also short, slim, and very quietly spoken, her mother Giovanna (my father's sister), her daughter Maria Grazia and step-daughter Giuseppina – both pretty young girls of about 12 years of age. The seven of us sat together around a large table in a rear room. Gina produced a couple of bottles of wine which I found particularly acceptable – being bombarded with questions in a language in which I was far from fluent made some sort of fortification most desirable.

When the hour came for the shop to be closed we all departed together and made our way on foot to the apartment in which Gina and her family lived – a very attractive home, some six floors up, with beautifully polished marble floors. Uncle Giovanni and I were invited to take a nap. We readily agreed and enjoyed an hour of blissful sleep. At about 8 o'clock we were awakened and offered glasses of Campari Soda prior to dinner. The dinner was superb and we ate, drank, and talked for two hours or more; there was a great deal of laughter as the girls made good-natured fun of my errors in speech and pronunciation and I was convulsed by their efforts to speak a few words in English.

It was altogether a very happy day for me. Eventually, as we were shown to our bedrooms, Gina informed me that the following day I would meet the rest of the family residing in Turin for a grand family gathering.

39. A Great Family Occasion

The following morning I was not awakened until late morning. I must have slept for almost ten hours. I knew that the previous days had exhausted me and I was grateful to Gina for not disturbing me. I felt refreshed and ready for what I knew would be an eventful day. Uncle Giovanni had also slept well and looked very sprightly. I had a bath, shaved and after several cups of coffee and some hot buttered toast I felt on top of the world. Mario possessed a small Fiat motor car and packed Gina and her mother, myself and Uncle Giovanni into the tiny vehicle to take us to the home of my Uncle Celestino, fortunately not too far away. During the journey Gina chattered away incessantly in her excitable manner, anxious to point out to me the various places of interest we were passing and pausing only to curse any motorist or pedestrian that dared to impede our progress! Maria Grazia and Giuseppina made the journey on foot.

When we arrived at our destination Celestino was waiting with his wife, my Aunt Ida. Celestino was a small wiry man and Ida a small but buxom woman. As I got out of the car, and released the other perspiring occupants, Celestino walked towards me – then held up his hand indicating me to halt. He gazed at me intently for a few seconds then proclaimed loudly, "Franco, Franco, sei veramente un Gianotti!" I gathered that he had perceived a family likeness and did not disapprove of what he saw. Then, before I could utter a word, he rushed forward and embraced me warmly, kissing me repeatedly on the cheeks. Ida repeated the process. Then my cousin Giovanni emerged from the house to introduce himself. Taller than his parents, and with a gold tooth that caught my eye, he greeted me equally warmly. We were all invited into the house and offered wine. At intervals other members of the family arrived; my Aunt Domenica, a spinster approaching 60 years of age but still slim and attractive; my Uncle Secondino, a quietly spoken bachelor; my Uncle Giulio and his wife Marfisa and, finally, my Godfather Pierino and his wife Maria (my Godmother and my father's sister). The arrival of my Godparents provided the most emotional moment of all. Twenty years had passed since my Baptism in Turin and they had not seen me during that time. Now they were overjoyed and both wept tears of joy as they greeted me. I immediately felt great affection for them both; Maria, in her fifties but still a beautiful and elegant woman, and Pierino, small and dark with twinkling eyes. For the next few hours I enjoyed the company of all my family, chatting with each of them in turn. The hubbub in the house was unbelievable and I was grateful for the attentiveness of my cousin Giovanni who, whenever I seemed to be flagging, topped up my glass of wine and provided me with sandwiches or cake to sustain me. I gathered that we were all to enjoy a family dinner later that evening and readily agreed to Uncle Celestino's suggestion that I should have an hour's 'siesta' during the afternoon to refresh myself. I was conducted to a bedroom where I enjoyed an hour of complete relaxation, quite oblivious to everything happening around me. That evening I found everybody still present and we all moved outside to a courtyard at the rear of the house where a large table had been set up so that all the family could be comfortably seated. The prospect of dining outside appealed to me, it was a fine warm evening and little lamps on the table produced a wonderfully intimate atmosphere. Giovanni's fiancée, Clotilde, had arrived and there were now eighteen people around the table! Several members of the family served soup and various other splendid local dishes, including cooked meats and some marvellous spaghetti and there was wine in abundance. The eating went on for some hours and I enjoyed myself immensely. It seemed like something from a Hollywood film and there were moments when I wondered if it was all a dream. How my mother would have enjoyed such an occasion! She could not have imagined what I was enjoying at this moment. These lovely people were not wealthy and were still suffering from the after-effects of the war but they had spared no expense to make this loving family welcome one of the most wonderful and fulfilling occasions of my life.

I was taken back to Gina's house very late that evening feeling very content. Before retiring to bed Gina told me of the programme for the next two days. "Tomorrow Maria Grazia and Giuseppina will show you around Turin and the day after tomorrow you will travel to Ivrea with Uncle Celestino to visit the remainder of the family." It was clear to me now that Gina was the hub around which the family in Turin revolved. I embraced her and expressed my profound gratitude for all she was doing for me.

40. I Discover Turin

I had a splendid day with Maria Grazia and Giuseppina, getting to know a little about the beautiful City of Turin. The girls were wonderfully patient and it was a relief to have a day with only two people to converse with. We took a rowing boat out on the River Po and visited the medieval village with which I was absolutely enchanted. Travelling on foot and using local transport we saw numerous beautiful churches and parks, castles and palaces. I had always imagined that Turin, being the home of the Fiat Motor Car Company, would be a rather grim industrial city. I was more than delighted with the reality – with the stunning spectacle of the Alps as a background it was a beautiful and romantic place which I found irresistible.

As we rested for a while in one lovely park to eat our sandwiches I thought of my mother, alone at home, and wondered what memories she would have of Turin. I vowed again that I would bring her back to Italy for a holiday when I was finally finished with army life.

At the end of a perfect day we returned home and enjoyed another of Gina's splendid dinners. I tried not to think of my unit in Ancona – I wanted this leave to last forever.

I was quite tired at the end of the day and retired to bed at a fairly early hour. I would need my strength for the following day. Gina had informed me that I would be travelling by bicycle to Ivrea early next morning with Uncle Celestino. After my last bicycle ride I was somewhat apprehensive about the journey!

41. By Bicycle to Ivrea and Back

After a light continental breakfast with Gina I walked to the house of my Uncle Celestino, not far away. He was bright and cheerful and ready for our journey. He had procured a bicycle for me that was ancient to say the least – no gear mechanism and a saddle that was very hard and uncomfortable. I noticed that his own bike was not much better, no point moaning I thought – if the old chap can manage the journey then I surely can. It was still early in the morning when we departed and we rode side by side through a part of Turin before turning north towards the Alps.

Celestino chatted away as we rode, giving me all kind of information about the countryside through which we were travelling. He informed me that he had several friends at places on our route where we might stop to rest briefly. He was over 60 years of age, small and slightly built but was obviously very strong and had no difficulty in keeping going at a good speed.

As the morning went on it began to get very hot and the glare from the dusty white roads of the countryside was strong. My backside was becoming quite sore and it was a relief when we came across a small roadside bar. "Fermiamo, Franco, per un bicchiere di Vino" announced Celestino, to my delight. The owner of the bar was sitting at a little table outside, in the shade of a tree. He greeted Celestino warmly and I was introduced. Glasses of red wine were poured and after a couple of these, for which, incidentally, we were not allowed to pay, I felt revived. After a while Celestino jumped to his feet "Andiamo Franco", he exclaimed and off we went.

We pedalled steadily through the beautiful countryside, the peasants waving cheerfully to us as we passed by, and I soaked up the atmosphere and thought of my Father who had spent the first years of his life in this part of Italy. We had not travelled many more miles when my Uncle announced again "Fermiamo, Franco, per un altro bicchiere!" We dismounted again at another roadside bar, and were again warmly greeted by the owner – more wine was consumed. By now I was feeling quite merry, the combination of hot sun and wine was formidable, but we were not finished yet, we made one more stop for yet another refresher and by this time I had become oblivious to the sore backside and my aching legs!

Eventually we reached the town of Ivrea and the home of my Uncle Guido, a very spacious and comfortable apartment in the centre of the town. As we got off our bicycles I am sure we were both slightly unsteady on our feet! We were greeted very warmly by my uncle, a genial stocky little man, his wife Ester and their son and daughter, my cousins Aldo and Nella – both about my age and of my stature. Aldo, very dapper and handsome, Nella a lovely young girl. After we had washed and rested for a while I learned much about how they had survived the war years. Aldo had only recently returned home from the mountains where he had seen action with the Italian partisans. During the next days I experienced what was for me a most wonderful period.

My Uncle had managed to keep his business going (manufacturing various glass products) and the family were obviously poised to recover swiftly from the effects of the war. Although food was not yet available in great abundance Ester performed miracles with what they had and I found my meals, cooked in local style, absolutely delicious.

Aldo and Nella spent long hours showing me around Ivrea with its Cathedral and castle and we enjoyed some happy hours swimming from rowing boats in the lovely lake of Sirio and walking in the nearby mountains. Celestino was content to relax at home in the company of my aunt and uncle.

I was very sad when the time came for me to leave Ivrea. Everybody wept profusely when we said our goodbyes and I was urged to return as soon as possible. My aunt Ester kissed and embraced me with great warmth and was reluctant to release me. I had difficulty in holding back my own tears.

We mounted our bicycles and set off for the return journey to Turin. The weather was still wonderful and again the heat motivated Celestino to call for halts for liquid refreshment at intervals! On the way back Celestino decided on a diversion so that we could visit the village of Borgo d'Ale where my father was born. He pointed out the actual house in which the family had lived. I was fascinated by the experience and had a strange sense of having been there before. "Probably the emotion and the effect of the wine", I told myself, but the feeling was to linger long afterwards. We eventually reached Turin late in the day and Celestino accompanied me to Gina's apartment where I was to spend a few more days before leaving for Milan, my Uncle Giovanni having already departed to return to his work. Gina greeted me warmly and was delighted to have news of our time in Ivrea and to know that my stay there had given me such pleasure.

Celestino by now was quite exhausted and, after thanking him repeatedly for his company and for all he had done for me, I persuaded him to return to his home. I, too, was feeling very tired and I was pleased at the prospect of another good night's sleep in a comfortable bed, between clean white sheets, a luxury to which I had not yet become fully reaccustomed.

42. Goodbye to Turin

The remaining days in Turin were occupied very happily by visits to all the members of the family in their own homes, for a final farewell. I was wined and dined royally and made to feel very much at home. The most emotional of these occasions was the visit to my Godparents Pierino and Maria. They lived in a tiny apartment high up in a block of flats not far from the centre of Turin, sparsely furnished but kept sparkling clean and tidy. They were obviously far from wealthy but spared no expense to provide a fine meal and good wine. They talked at length about my father and mother and gave a detailed account of the events that took place on the occasion of my baptism in Turin. I felt very close to this lovely frail old couple and was made to promise to return with my mother at the earliest possible moment. I left them, both smiling through their tears, with a lump in my throat and a heavy heart. My round of visits continued until I had said goodbye to everybody, individually. I felt totally a part of a loving family.

The time I had spent in Milan, Turin and Ivrea was the happiest period of my life so far. Also I felt a great personal sense of achievement. My father had been one of a family of eleven and I had now found all his brothers and sisters, except for Davide who died in the First World War and Pietro who had gone to live in France in 1902 and with whom all contact has ceased.

I had also been made aware of the wonderful family relationships that the Italians have and had been showered with every kindness and great love by every member of the family. My great regret was that I had nothing to offer in return for all that I had received. I could only hope that some day in the future, when my life in England started again, I would be able to entertain members of the family from Italy and endeavour to reciprocate their wonderful hospitality.

Finally the time came for me to leave Turin for Milan. Gina, Mario and the girls accompanied me to the railway station and they all wept and embraced me warmly as I boarded the train. I felt hugely indebted to them and as I waved goodbye from the train window there were tears in my eyes.

The journey back to Milan was uneventful and I dozed off for short periods as the train chugged along, reflecting on the events of the days that had passed so quickly.

The whole period now seemed dreamlike and unreal. The joy that I had experienced during these days was almost indescribable, particularly as it followed years of wartime hardship; a long, long, period of deprivation and fear, a period when the future was uncertain and survival was the main aim in life. Now there was light at the end of the tunnel and I felt that this wonderful period of leave was the start of better things to come.

43. Back to Ancona and Army Life

When the train reached the Milan railway station I made my way back to my Uncle's apartment on foot. Giovanni and his sister-in-law were there, waiting for me. They greeted me warmly and told me that they had arranged a special meal for me that evening and that Ottavio would also be present. They knew that I would be leaving them on the following morning to return to my army unit in Ancona and were eager to have all the news concerning my time in Turin and Ivrea. During dinner I told them, in detail, of all that had happened. They were relieved that I had returned safely and delighted to know that everything had gone so smoothly. They could see how overjoyed I was to have been able to meet all the members of my Italian family and were very gratified. The meal was splendid and much wine was enjoyed. Zio Giovanni, with his sparkling dry sense of humour, was in great form and there was much laughter, especially when I recounted details of my bicycle ride to Ivrea with Zio Celestino! Occasionally I had to urge them to slow down so that I could fully understand what was being said but, in the main, I was able to follow all the conversation quite well.

Eventually the time came to retire and as I climbed into the white-sheeted comfortable bed I reflected, with some sadness, that I would not be enjoying this luxury again in the foreseeable future. It was after midnight and I was by now very tired. Aided no doubt by the amount of wine I had consumed I fell into a deep sleep. When I awoke it was turned eight o'clock and I hurriedly washed and shaved to be ready for departure. After a light breakfast and several cups of black coffee I got my bits and pieces into my backpack and my uncle accompanied me to the street below. In a short time I had become very fond of him; I thanked him profusely for his marvellous hospitality and did my best to smile but the parting was quite painful for me. He was very emotional about my departure and I assured him that I would return as soon as possible.

"Arrividerci, caro Franco, buon viaggio e buona fortuna", he said, then he embraced me warmly – tears streaming down his cheeks.

"Arrividerci, caro Zio", I replied, then left him and commenced my journey with a heavy heart.

The return to Ancona was achieved without any difficulties. I obtained a lift from a civilian in a private car for the first part of the journey and thereafter from several army vehicles. I had decided to make for Bologna, reached the town by early evening and found the army transit camp again. I produced the letter from my CO and was told that I could stay the night. By now my money had nearly run out and I settled for a free army meal – very basic after the food I had been enjoying over the last fortnight but welcome nevertheless. I did not sleep well that night. My mind was constantly churning over all that had happened in two short weeks and the musty-smelling palliasse on a hard wooden bed was not too comfortable, although I was grateful for a place to spend the night. The following morning I got up with the lark, shaved and washed and then drifted down to the mess with some other lads in transit. I had quite a good breakfast during which I had the good fortune to encounter an ambulance driver who would be leaving for Rimini in an hour or so. He offered me a lift and I gratefully accepted. At Rimini I decided that, as I was now well up to schedule, I would walk down to the beach. I found myself a quiet spot, took off my jacket, shirt and boots and lazed in the sunshine, listening to the sound of the calm Adriatic gently lapping upon the shore. I dozed off intermittently for an hour or so after which I freshened myself up, washing my face and feet in seawater. Afterwards, back on the main road running parallel to the sea, I hitched another lift, taking me to Senigallia. It was evening and I was now very hungry. I found a little trattoria and ordered eggs and chips and a half bottle of wine. As I sat quietly enjoying my meal three soldiers entered. They were obviously on a night out and drank heavily. I became involved in conversation and enjoyed a drink or two with them – time passed quickly. I had decided to use every moment of my leave and not return to my unit prematurely but I was now cutting things very fine; I left in haste and was again fortunate in quickly obtaining a lift to the port of Ancona. I arrived back at camp at 23.45 and booked in at the guardroom – 15 minutes before my deadline. I had no money whatsoever left in my pockets! Watcham and Riley were awake when I reached our quarters and greeted me warmly. "Nice to have you back 'G', we've missed you." We chatted for a few minutes before we were made aware that we were disturbing our comrades. "It's that noisy little bastard Gianotti", came one voice. Another bawled "Jump on his head somebody and let's get to sleep". More pleasantries followed! Not wishing to invite any further terms of endearment, or worse, I put out the light. I was back to army life!

44. Robbed in Bari

Apart from exercises in training I had managed to get through my army life so far without having to defend myself or use the violent methods of combat instructed in training. This happy state of affairs came to an end one morning in Bari, in Southern Italy.

I was returning North after a period away from my unit (having been on detachment for a period to a company in Southern Italy) accompanied by another driver, one James Potts. I pulled up in a main street not far from the centre of the town to make a purchase at a shop. My kitbag was in the cab at the front of the vehicle.

"Keep an eye on my kit, Jim," I said. "I won't be gone more than a minute or so."

When I returned James was standing by the side of the truck, eyeing up some local girls. As I opened the cab door my heart missed a beat – my kitbag, containing most of my worldly possessions had gone!

"What's happened," I asked James "Have you put the kitbag in the back of the truck?" Before he could reply an old lady who was standing nearby tugged at my arm.

"Ladri, tre ladri," she shouted excitedly. Then she pointed to a narrow street on the other side of the road into which the three thieves had disappeared. I knew I had to move quickly.

"Stay here with the truck Jim," I shouted, and then raced across the road. The street was marked with 'No Go' signs, indicating that allied troops were forbidden to enter. Impulsively I ignored them and ran on blindly. As I got deeper and deeper into the forbidden zone I had an amazing piece of luck, I came across a small square in which, unbelievably, obviously thinking they had reached a secure place, the thieves were standing over my opened kitbag. There were two young ragamuffins, both only about ten years of age, and a big swarthy-looking man who had opened up my precious camera and was examining it. Impetuously I ran towards them shouting "Ladri, ladri!"

The two urchins panicked and ran off, dropping the garments they had removed from the kitbag as they fled. The big man stood his ground and foolishly I tried to seize the camera from his grasp but only succeeded in sending it falling to the ground. He aimed a punch at me, his fist crashing against the side of my head, and I staggered backwards. His hand was heavy with rings and there was a trickle of blood from a cut above my eyebrow. As he came at me again I knew I was in real trouble against a much bigger and heavier adversary. No time for Marquis of Queensbury rules here – as he threw his second punch I swayed sideways, taking hold of his coat sleeve and jerking him off-balance. In the same movement I brought up my right leg and jabbed the steel-tipped heel of my army boot into his groin with all the force I could muster. The ruffian fell heavily to the ground, groaning in agony, and as I saw the pain on his face I knew there would be no further aggression. By now several other locals had arrived on the scene and, fearful that they might be hostile, I hastily gathered up the camera and the other items scattered around and threw them into the kitbag. Then I had a further stroke of good fortune – a carabinieri arrived on the scene, just as the villain had got to his feet and limped away. I explained what had happened.

"You shouldn't be in this zone you know," he pointed out. "You could have put yourself in grave danger."

He wasn't telling me anything I didn't know! Without further ado he escorted me back to the truck and the sight of it was a great relief to me. James was sitting inside, at the steering wheel. He glanced at the kitbag, slung over my shoulder.

"You've got it back then," he observed. The remark seemed so utterly naïve, so matter of fact, that it caused me great irritation.

"Yes, I've got it back you stupid peasant," I growled, "And I bloody well nearly got done in the process!"

He noticed the cut over my eye and blood seeping from it.

"Sorry 'G," he said, "I'm very glad you've got back safely".

I thanked the policeman for his assistance and without further delay we continued our journey. As the miles went by the ache in my head subsided and I recovered my composure. I reflected on how I had been forced to adopt desperate measures in self-defence, using violence contrary to my nature, and I derived no satisfaction from my success apart from the relief of recovering my possessions.

It was not the first time that I had acted on impulse in a difficult situation and I was thankful that I had again emerged relatively unscathed. I had been very lucky. In future I would be more careful.

45. Like Ducks to Water!

In July 1945 I found myself back in Southern Italy with a number of drivers from my company, including my good friends Arthur Watcham and Sid Riley. We were housed in tents on the beach at Salerno and were to receive training on the amphibious vehicles known as Ducks (officially designated as DUKW'S). Initially we viewed this development with approval and, indeed, derived great pleasure from driving these huge vehicles around the streets in and around Salerno and experiencing the exhilaration of driving from dry land straight into the sea. Once one became accustomed to the method of handling these huge unwieldy vehicles there were no real problems and the days passed very agreeably on the sun-baked beaches. Furthermore, there was plenty of free time in which to enjoy the odd glass of wine in the various bars throughout the town and we were able to get day passes enabling us to visit such places as Sorrento, Amalfi and Positano on the beautiful Neapolitan Riviera coast, the San Carlo Opera House in Naples, and the wonderful excavations at the city of Pompeii.

It always seemed extraordinary to me that wherever we were in Italy, with so many marvellous places within relatively easy reach, the majority of our troops seemed to prefer to make for the nearest NAAFI forces canteen. In our new location, during a conversation with Sid, I commented on this fact.

"You know, Sid, we've been very lucky to get through the war unscathed. We are enjoying things now that would have been beyond the reach of the average chap before the war. If we've got to be stuck in the army for another year or so let's make the most of it."

Sid was in a glum mood, probably due to his guard duty the night before.

"You're right 'G'", he observed, "but don't get too carried away – the bloody war with Japan isn't over yet and this training will make us perfectly suited for the operations in the Far East."

I pondered on this very unpalatable prognosis for a second or so, then decided to forget the subject.

"Cheer up Sid, for God's sake. Let's find a nice little bar and enjoy a bevy. We'll drink to the joys of the moment!"

The very mention of a drink or two had a wonderfully beneficial effect on my friend and the little binge that followed removed all pessimistic notions, at least temporarily, from his mind. His morale improved perceptibly! Such moments of happy escapism occurred periodically in a soldier's life; they made the whole business much more bearable.

46. The End of the War with Japan

After the 'Duck' training had been completed and my group had returned to company HQ in Ancona the normal truck-driving routine continued.

Life was fairly pleasant and each day my assignments took me to new and interesting places. The main concern now, however, for all the troops was for news of the war with Japan. After years of bitter fighting throughout the whole of the far-eastern theatres of war the Japanese army, navy and air-forces had suffered a chain of defeats at the hands of the American and allied forces. On April 1st 1945 the Americans had landed in Okinawa – one of the islands between Formosa and Japan. It seemed that the end must be near. Then, on August 6th 1945 came sensational and totally unexpected news – the Americans had dropped the first atomic bomb on the Japanese city of Hiroshima! It was later reported that the bomb (bearing the bizarre name 'Little Boy') was a uranium bomb and that it had destroyed most of the city and killed about 80,000 people – almost a quarter of the population! Three days later, on August 9th, 'Fat Man', a plutonium bomb, was dropped on the city of Nagasaki also inflicting terrible destruction and causing appalling loss of life.

The use of these terrible new weapons of war hastened the end for the Japanese, who had been close to defeat before their use, and on August 14th 1945 the Japanese surrender was made. There was a great debate as to whether it was necessary for these atomic bombs to be used. The American view was that to finish the war by conventional methods would have incurred even greater loss of life – there was no argument from our troops who rejoiced and said prayers of thanksgiving – now at last it was all over. I felt a great feeling of relief; it was now unlikely that my comrades and I would be moved to another continent. Now we must all patiently wait for demobilization and a return to our families and, hopefully, to a peaceful world. It would not happen quickly. The occupying armies would remain in place in Italy and Germany for a long time to come. It was predicted that it would take a year or two before demobilization was completed. Never mind; men like myself who had survived one of the most terrible wars in history and were physically unscathed had been very fortunate and the period ahead should not be too hard to endure. What would be in store for us now?

47. I Become a Sea Captain!

In the latter half of August 1945 I observed an unusual announcement on the company notice board reading 'Volunteers required for a period of duty with RASC (Water Transport) Company'. I was intrigued, made a brief enquiry, then mentioned the announcement to my good friends Arthur and Sid.

"Let's have a powwow over a beer tonight," I suggested.

The idea of consuming a little wine was never unacceptable to these two and we met that evening in a nearby bar. "Look you chaps," I said, "this could be just the thing we need. I understand that the job consists of looking after ships transporting supplies to Adriatic ports. It would be a marvellous break from our daily routine with a good deal of freedom – no guard duties or company discipline. It's only for a month or two and we would be working with Italian seamen which I think would be quite a lark. Shall we have a go?"

They were both in accord and the following morning we each handed in our names to company office.

There was no delay and two days later we packed our kitbags and were transported south by truck to Molfetta – a pretty little Adriatic fishing port just above the major port of Bari. There was an army sergeant on duty at the port to whom we were instructed to report. Apparently he worked in conjunction with the Navy and the Port Authorities and he gave us our briefing:-
"You lads are here to act as escorts on vessels manned by Italian crews. You are relieving men who are either going home on leave or to be demobilized. You will go individually to your respective ships on which you will live for the entire period of

your stay. You will eat and sleep on your vessels and will draw rations from stores in whatever port you happen to be located. The ships are old diesel-powered schooners of around 300 tons and are all currently in this port. You will be responsible for the loading and delivery of cargoes and generally to keep your crews in order. Most of them are splendid men and your predecessors managed well. It helps if you can speak Italian, of course, and if you don't get seasick!" Sid, who had been quiet until now, looked a little stunned. Obviously he had not realised the full extent of the job.

"Bloody hell 'G'! What have you got us into?"

"Not to worry, Sid," I replied, "you'll soon pick up the language and it will be plain sailing – you'll love it!"

He didn't look too convinced.

"I'll teach the buggers English!" he snapped, in the true fashion of British troops abroad.

After arranging to meet the others later I was the first to be taken by the sergeant to my ship. It was not as I imagined. It stood high in the water with a tall mast, a rather antiquated wheelhouse in the bow and a curious box-style cabin on the centre of the deck. As we approached a man jumped from the deck onto the quay to greet us. The sergeant introduced us.

"This is Captain Antenore" he announced. The captain, a lean and handsome man in his middle years, greeted me with a warm smile and a firm handshake. "He speaks very little English" said the sergeant. I glanced at the captain and introduced myself.

"Buona sera Capitano, mi chiamo Gianotti, Franco Gianotti."

He was delighted to learn that I could converse in his language and, bidding the sergeant goodbye, we climbed aboard. As soon as we were on deck the crew appeared. I observed immediately that they were an assortment of marvellous characters. The captain introduced me to them, one at a time: "Luigi Rozzi – Motorista" (middle-aged, stocky and swarthy, with a gold tooth that gave him a devilish look when he smiled). "Roberto – Il Cuoco" (elderly but still handsome with dark, curly hair and a warm smile). "Pietro – Motorista" (very dark and serious looking). "Mariano – Marinaio" and "Augusto – Marinaio" (two cheerful-looking seamen who both smiled constantly). "Ennio – Ragazzo" (this dark, deeply tanned ship's boy was, in fact, the cook's son). "Reginaldo – Marinaio" (the 'old man' of the crew, wrinkled and gnarled, a real old sea dog). Finally the last crew member was introduced "Giovanni – Il Nostromo" (tall, dark and very handsome, in his twenties, I was impressed with the bosun's striking good looks and proud bearing. As I shook his hand I felt that here I would have a good friend).

Struggling hard to remember all the names, I was led by the captain to my quarters – I was to occupy the cabin on the deck. There was a bunk on either side, with blankets on each bunk, and although fairly primitive I was quite pleased with the situation. At least I would be on my own whenever I wished to be, and would be able to sleep undisturbed. I unpacked my kitbag and put my bits and pieces away. The captain then took me below deck to show me where meals were served and to offer me a glass of wine which I readily accepted.

He raised his glass, "Buona fortuna Signor Franco".

"Buona fortuna Capitano Antenore" I responded. We had an hour or so before our dinner would be ready and I took the opportunity to leave the ship and familiarise myself with the surrounding area. As I did so I glanced back at the vessel and observed the name, obviously recently changed, on the ship's side – "ITALIA LIBERATA".

I had a feeling that I might find this new and strange period of service life very enjoyable. It would certainly be different! I wondered how Arthur and Sid were faring. It would be a little more difficult for them. I was not unduly concerned, they were both very adaptable and I was certain that they, too, would enjoy this new experience. I would find out soon enough, none of the ships would be leaving port that night. That evening I met my two friends, each on his own ship; the conditions were much the same as on my vessel and the Italian seamen had greeted them both in a very friendly manner. I was relieved and could see that they would have no great difficulty in coping with these new and most unusual circumstances. I ascertained from the sergeant that we would be working the same ports and would be meeting each other frequently. This news was received with smiles by Arthur and Sid. We agreed that whoever first sighted one of the others in any port would fly an army sock from the mast! This ritual was carried out several times in the weeks that followed – with all due solemnity – much to the amusement of the crews!

My first days aboard ship were wonderful. Gradually I got to know each member of the crew and I experienced a feeling of being 'one of the family', to such an extent that my early feelings of loneliness on being separated from my army comrades were completely dispelled. The food was unbelievably good – especially appreciated after years of army cooking. I ate light meals in my cabin or on deck during the day. At about seven o'clock each evening I had dinner below deck with the crew. Roberto (the cook) had experienced service on transatlantic liners prior to the war and his cooking was marvellous. There was splendid conversation and at each meal the wine flowed freely.

The days passed pleasantly as we moved supplies from one port to another – generally fairly short voyages along the Adriatic coast. My own duties were simple; I made contact with the appropriate officer at each port, checked the loading and unloading of cargoes, kept a log recording departure and arrival times and other simple ship's details. Apart from these tasks there was little to do but enjoy the pleasure of being on a ship, in wonderful sunny weather. I was quite comfortable in my little cabin and, once I had become accustomed to the constant movement on the sea, I slept like a log each night.

When in port, awaiting loading or unloading, I was completely free to come and go as I wished and I revelled in the opportunity to explore the quaint little ports and imagined how an artist would savour the picturesque scenes and brilliant colour found everywhere. On-board ship Ennio and I had become friends. The boy acted as a sort of 'batman' for me and did my washing and ironing regularly. At times I had to pinch myself to be assured that this was not a dream and then reflected, sadly, that this sublime existence would not continue indefinitely. I made up my mind that I would enjoy every day as it came, for as long as the idyll lasted!

I was very thankful that I had recovered my camera with my other possessions at the time of the robbery in Bari. With it I was able to take photographs of the "Italia Liberata" and the crew. I knew that when I finally got back to civilian life, and my memory faded with the passing years, these photographs would prove that the whole period had been a reality. They would enable me to re-live what was to be a very happy and, in the main, tranquil period of my life – and a unique experience.

48. Fouling Up the Adriatic!

On a morning in late August, back in the port of Ancona, I reported as usual for a new assignment.

"We've got something unusual for you," said the sergeant in charge, "You'll be dumping some ammunition at sea – a cargo of bloody big shells to be exact". In the army I had learned to be prepared for the unexpected but this was something out of the ordinary! The sergeant continued "There will be some trucks coming in shortly, we have arranged for Swazi labour troops to do the loading and they will sail with you and chuck the lot overboard at a specified position – well out to sea. With any luck you should be back this evening".

Within minutes the vehicles arrived, carrying half a dozen black soldiers. They loaded the shells, placing them side by side on the deck. Without undue delay we left the harbour and headed for the open sea. It was not a mission that gave me any pleasure; shortly after leaving port the weather deteriorated and the sea became choppy. The shells started to roll across the deck and I was uneasy about the instability of this strange cargo, furthermore the troops on board looked very queasy and there was much moaning and groaning as the ship rolled from side to side. Some of them became seasick and puked over the side and I was very relieved when the captain informed me that we had reached the dumping area. At first the men were reluctant to start work and I had to urge them into action. "If you don't start soon we'll be out here all bloody night – and we'll stay here until the job is done!" This did the trick and, with much grunting, swearing and lurching about on the heaving deck, the deadly cargo was tossed overboard, piece by piece. For a few minutes I stood reflecting on this strange scene – yet another example of the madness of war. I thought of the men and women who had laboured night and day in factories, doubtless often during air raids, to produce these munitions, of the sailors who had risked their lives to deliver them, and of the fact that some of these shells might even have been transported by me to the ammunition dump from which they had been consigned that morning! Now, after so much endeavour, they would find a resting place on the bed of the Adriatic Sea. What the effect, if any, would be on the environment in years to come I could not imagine. I doubted whether anybody had given this too much thought. With the mission completed I gave the soldiers a few cigarettes each and, happy to be back on dry land, they departed in a much better frame of mind.

I had some film left in my camera and, despite the upheaval during this operation, had been able to take a few photographs to provide a record of what had been a most bizarre day in the life of a soldier!

49. Across The Adriatic

After a day or so of relaxation in Ancona, spent happily in the company of a few of the younger crew members and during which I enjoyed some wonderful bathing in the warm Adriatic Sea, I was advised that we were to take on board a cargo of supplies destined for the port of Pola[2] on the eastern side of the Adriatic and occupied by the British. We loaded promptly and left without delay. The voyage across was uneventful and I kept busy writing a long letter to my mother detailing my adventures during the recent weeks. As we got near to the port Ennio knocked on the door of my cabin and called excitedly, "Franco, Franco, vieni presto!" He passed me a pair of binoculars and pointed to a particular section of the harbour. When I got the glasses into focus I jumped for joy – berthed in the harbour was Watcham's schooner with a sock dangling from the mast! Within a few minutes we arrived at the quayside. To my delight there stood Arthur, beaming.

"Great to see you G", he said, "I got to hear you were coming in and I've got a bottle ready on my boat".

On board his ship he gave me a full account of what he had been doing. He was liked by his crew and, like myself, found the life at sea very agreeable.

"Listen G", he said "I've chummed up with a naval chap who gets his hands on a jeep without too much difficulty. You'll be free tomorrow and if we buy him a drink or two and some grub he'll show us the sights." I was enthusiastic about this prospect. The following day, after we had unloaded our cargo,

---

[2] Italian since 1919, Pola (now Pula) was given to Yugoslavia in the peace treaty of 1947.

the naval chap turned up and the tour commenced. The little seaport of Pola with its large deep harbour was situated at the southern end of the peninsula of Istria. The town was much smaller than I had imagined but, we soon discovered, was rich in history.

There were some amazing Roman remains, including a wonderful arena in a very good state of preservation, a temple, and some original Roman Gates. These were all visited in turn and were described by our naval friend as if he was a professional tour guide. We two soldiers, indeed, sat imperiously upright in the jeep, taking in every word and assuming the postures of wealthy tourists! When the touring was over we found a little trattoria where we enjoyed a decent meal and a good deal of wine. We were driven back to our ships by our naval friend. Before he left us he warned "Be careful not to stray outside the town – things are far from settled in these parts and there are some dangerous people about". We were in too happy a frame of mind for this to cause us too much concern at that moment!

50. Unfriendly Yugoslavs in Parenzo

Our stay in Pola was very brief, both my own schooner and Watcham's were detailed to carry consignments of building materials to Trieste. I was to leave the day before him. When the time came to leave he turned up to see us off and cheerfully waved to us from the quayside. I had enjoyed our short time together immensely.

As we left the sheltered harbour I noticed that the skies had darkened and that a strong breeze was blowing. We turned north, heading for Trieste. About half-way to our destination the weather worsened and the ship began to roll alarmingly. I stood on deck, hanging on to anything that was securely fixed, with the spray lashing my face. Shortly the captain called to me.

"Franco, these conditions were not expected. The 'Bora' is blowing from the north east and it will be dangerous to try to continue". He pointed to the land on our starboard side, and continued, "Over there is the port of Parenzo. I think we must seek shelter there until tomorrow, by which time conditions should improve". I was in total agreement, and we changed course immediately, much to my relief.

Immediately after we had entered the port a motor launch sped out to meet us and its three occupants came on board – Yugoslav soldiers, presumably with port duties – swarthy, evil-looking, unkempt individuals with pistols, knives and ammunition belts hung about them. A more fearsome-looking trio one could not imagine! They demanded to know what our cargo was and where we were bound. None of them spoke English but fortunately they understood Italian. They were curious to know why an English soldier was working with a crew of Italian seamen and, with the Captain's assistance, I was able to explain. It was a situation in which I felt uncomfortable and I was rather thankful that they did not find our cargo at all interesting. After a while they departed, unsmiling and unfriendly, after making it clear that neither I nor the Captain and crew would be welcome ashore.

Later that afternoon a rowing boat came alongside. Aboard were two Italians, young men – probably in their mid-twenties. After a brief conversation with the Captain and me, from the side of the ship, they were invited to come on board. They painted a grim picture of conditions in the area.

"There is no rule of law – robberies, rapes and murders occur frequently and victims are thrown into unmarked shallow graves. We live in fear".

I tried to introduce a more cheerful tone into the conversation.

"The war has not been over for very long. Perhaps things will be better soon and life will return to normal."

The reply from one was immediate.

"Life will never be normal again. There are too many guns, too many religions, too many bitter memories, too much hatred. One day the whole of Yugoslavia will be engulfed in a terrible civil war".

I did not know then how deadly accurate this prophesy would prove to be.

I managed to persuade one of the young men to return briefly to land, to procure some postcards for me depicting Parenzo. Shortly afterwards they departed, two sad figures, but very grateful for some chocolate and cigarettes I had given them.

It was now late and very dark. Captain Antenore agreed with me that we should have a man on watch for two-hour spells during the night. I was in melancholy mood and did not sleep well, being aware of the creaking of the ship and the sounds of the sea until dawn came.

In the morning the weather was much improved, with sunshine and a calmer sea. We departed in haste and headed north for Trieste, where the British were in control and which I was sure would be a more hospitable place.

51. Fun and Games in Trieste and Venice

Trieste, the largest seaport on the Adriatic, was being administered by the Allied Military Government and when we arrived there I was very impressed by the size of the port and its shipyards. It had been heavily bombed during the war but now seemed to be returning to normal. Luigi, the 'Motorista', knew the city well and promised to show me around it if time permitted.

We unloaded our cargo on the day of arrival and, to my delight, there were no instructions for our next assignment, with the prospect of perhaps a few days of free time.

Watcham's schooner arrived that afternoon and his situation seemed to be similar. The following morning Luigi kept his promise and took the pair of us on a guided tour starting at the Faro della Vittoria – the great lighthouse at the northern end of the harbour – and continuing for some hours through a large part of the city.

Beneath Luigi's rough exterior lurked a very intelligent and likeable man. He was quite happily married, but when away from his home port he had a weakness for female company. In this respect he took us, at the end of our tour, to a little 'trattoria' on the outskirts of the city where he hoped to find an old female acquaintance. Sure enough she was there – a raven-haired buxom woman of very generous proportions, with a flashing smile. She was seated, sipping a Cinzano, but leapt to her feet as we arrived and embraced Luigi warmly. He introduced us to her.

"Questa e Lucia, mia fidanzata," he announced with a twinkle in his eye. She kissed each of us warmly on both cheeks. From the way in which she was dressed and her general manner it seemed probable that she was not employed at the restaurant but had another profession! After enjoying a glass of wine with us all Luigi made his apologies and departed with Lucia, leaving Watcham and myself in the company of the owner of the 'Trattoria'. We chatted for a while and then, quite unexpectedly, two young women came bustling in.

Obviously they were known to the proprietor and he introduced them to us. They were very attractive girls, probably in their early twenties. Both were able to speak a little English and seemed pleased to have our company. They suggested that we might meet again. Watcham's face lit up! It was a long time since he had last been out with a girl.

"G", he said, "We've struck oil!"

We quickly established a friendship and met them again several times in the days that followed. The highlight of this period came on a Sunday, when we managed to obtain some motor transport to take the four of us to and from Venice, which was not too far distant. There, in one of the world's most romantic places, we enjoyed the sort of day one might have only dreamed about – visits to the Doge's Palace, the Bridge of Sighs, drinks in St Mark's Square and, finally, a trip in two gondolas. So soon after the war there were not yet many tourists about – just military people from all nations.

As we glided, side by side through the canals of Venice, I called across to Watcham, "Make the most of this Arthur – when we're back in civvy street it will be years and years before you'll be able to afford anything like this!"

We took some photographs to prove to the lads back in Ancona that it had been possible for two ordinary soldiers to have enjoyed this kind of heaven!

It was all too good to last; after a few precious days both our ships took on cargoes destined for ports further south. We said our goodbyes to the girls and departed from Trieste, promising to return and taking very pleasant memories with us.

52. A Sad Goodbye to my Ship

My last days aboard the 'Italia Liberata' were spent ferrying supplies between various ports on the Southern Adriatic coast. By now I had formed firm friendships with every member of the crew, particularly with Captain Antenore[3], Luigi Rozzi, Giovanni the bosun, and the boy Ennio. The latter was meticulous in keeping my cabin spotlessly clean and tidy and my clothes were always clean and neatly pressed. During the day I busied myself helping the crew members with their tasks, after my own duties had been carried out. Although we were now into autumn the weather was still very good, with the days warm and sunny, and I enjoyed regular swimming from the beautiful Adriatic beaches with one or more members of the crew. In the evenings, after dinner with the crew, I would often remain with them, drinking a glass or two of wine, or playing cards. On several occasions I came across Sid Riley and Arthur Watcham and each meeting would result in a joyful celebration! Both these lads were completely adjusted to this new lifestyle, much to my relief and delight. The life aboard ship seemed to suit each of us. We were all very fit, deeply tanned, and not at all eager to rejoin our unit.

The days passed very quickly and I seemed to be living in a state of blissful euphoria when, finally, like all the best things in life, it all came to an end.

Our period of duty with the water transport company was abruptly ended as the original escorts returned. The time to leave had arrived. On the morning of my departure from the

[3] Over 20 years later, during a holiday in Italy with my family, I found Captain Antenore again, in his home town of Civitanova, near Ancona.

ship I cleared out my cabin and packed my possessions into my kitbag and backpack. The crew assembled on deck to say goodbye to me. I think that, mainly because I had integrated so happily into the ship's routine, I had earned their respect and affection. They were quite an emotional group of men and were very sorry to see me depart.

Ennio showed his feelings more than the others. As I embraced him he could hardly speak.

"Arrividerci Signor Franco – ritornare presto", he urged.

The words almost choked in his throat and tears streamed down his cheeks.

I appreciated his sentiments but knew that, in reality, it was very unlikely that we would ever meet again. I shook hands and embraced each man and then stepped off the side of the ship, waving to them as I did so. I found it difficult to control my own emotions. It was an infinitely sad parting. During the period spent with them I had experienced a totally new way of life and had been shown great understanding and kindness. My life had been enriched by my experiences aboard the ship in the company of such a fine crew.

I would never forget that happy group of men and would always treasure the memories of my time aboard the 'Italia Liberata'.

53. Back to the Old Routine

After the wonderful period aboard ship it was hard to adjust again to normal army life in Ancona, but there were some compensations. I was, on several occasions, fortunate to be given some long distance convoy work taking me to Milan and Turin. On these occasions, sometimes accompanied by one or more of my fellow soldiers, I was able to skive off and call briefly on my Uncle Giovanni in Milan, my cousin Gina in Turin, and my Uncle Guido in Ivrea. On each visit I was warmly received, as were the soldiers who accompanied me. Then, after a few weeks had passed, I was moved, with a group, back to Caserta in Southern Italy. My good friends Sid Riley and Arthur Watcham were still with me and we managed to get to Naples together on several occasions. During this period, together with another driver, I had a very unusual series of assignments:-

The newspaper produced especially for the forces and titled 'The Union Jack' was being printed in Rome. Together with a co-driver the work involved driving up to Rome, spending the night in army accommodation there and in the evening, after a free day in Rome, collecting the freshly printed edition. Driving through the night we then transported thousands of copies back south and made deliveries to various destinations. This work went on for some time and, although the roads were not good and the routine very tiring, the free days in Rome were a wonderful bonus and I got to know that beautiful city quite well, making visits to St Peter's, the Coliseum, the Roman Forum, the Catacombs and other places of great interest to me. There was a special magic for me about the eternal city and I was sorry when we were replaced by drivers from another unit and these assignments came to an end.

It had been a memorable period for me, particularly as I had been connected with newspapers once again, although only remotely. I wondered how long it would be before I would resume my civilian connection with the newspaper business with a pen as my tool instead of a three ton truck!

54. A Move to a New Company In Padua

After long periods spent in Southern Italy the time arrived for a transfer to a new company and, with Sid Riley, Arthur Watcham and a dozen or so of my other friends, I was to be posted to a GHQ car company stationed in Padua. We were all rather sorry to be leaving so many of our comrades, with whom we had soldiered for so long, but at the same time were pleased at the prospect of moving to a new and interesting location. On the last evening together we enjoyed a rather splendid goodbye party, attended by all our friends.

The following morning, with bleary eyes and aching heads, we were transported north. When we arrived in Padua we were delivered to our new home – a very ancient building which, we were informed, had been a monastery. The rooms in which we were to live were large and cold, mostly without window panes, but at least we had a roof over our heads and there was the possibility of visits to nearby Venice on off-duty days and, for me especially, perhaps the chance to get to Milan and Turin again and visit my relatives. This I achieved on several occasions, always receiving a splendid welcome.

The period was not otherwise eventful except for one rather unpleasant experience... There had been several disturbances in the Padua area between political groups and for various reasons some hostility had been shown to allied troops. While driving a fairly high-ranking Army officer through the centre of the town, in a beautiful Humber 'Snipe' I observed a large crowd of civilians beginning to fill the road ahead. They were carrying pieces of wood, bricks etc and generally looked very hostile. There was no room in which to turn the car around. I glanced at my passenger for an instruction.

"Put your foot hard on the pedal, Gianotti, and go like bloody hell," he bawled.

I had already decided on that exact course of action and, needing no second telling, stood hard on the accelerator, at the same time sounding a continuous ear-shattering blast on the horn. The powerful vehicle surged forward and the effect on the crowd was magical – like the parting of the Red Sea, I thought for one fleeting moment! As we hurtled through, bricks, bottles and pieces of wood rained down on the car and I was much relieved when we reached the safety of the clear road ahead. I do not believe that I inflicted injuries on any members of the mob and knew that we had taken the only sensible course of action. To stop the vehicle and try to reason with them would probably have been suicidal, especially as we had no indication of why they were so hostile.

I glanced again at my passenger.

"Well done, Gianotti," he remarked, in a somewhat subdued tone. I noticed that he was sweating profusely!

Safely back at camp I reflected again on how very fortunate I had been to survive my army service without suffering any serious physical injury. I thought, also, how ironic it would have been, at this late stage of the game, if I had been harmed by Italians – for whom I always had nothing but respect and affection.

I was now not too far off my demobilisation day and this brief episode made me doubly aware of the need for caution and self-preservation in the days ahead.

55. A Glimpse of Paradise

In early 1947 I was once again on the move, again on detachment from my Company, this time moved back south to Naples with three other drivers. We were billeted in a very ancient castle on the fringe of the city and, using staff cars and one truck, would be providing all the transport requirements for an outfit, the existence of which I had not previously known, described as 'The Yugoslav Screening Commission'. The officers serving in this organisation had the task of screening displaced persons. They were all likeable, highly intelligent men, specially trained for the job and on meeting them I formed the opinion that the routine would be interesting, with a bare minimum of the usual soul-destroying, boring military routine.

The accommodation in the castle was very basic – the customary wooden beds, with straw-filled palliasses, were situated in large draughty rooms with stone floors – not very inviting and very cold. We soon adjusted to this new, rather strange, environment and I personally was fascinated by the place which apparently had a remarkable history.

The work of the commission kept all the vehicles in constant use, taking us to different parts of Southern Italy, mainly in the vicinity of Naples. On several occasions I entered the prison there, where the officers interrogated suspected war criminals. Conditions in the prison were appalling and on each occasion I felt a great sense of relief as I emerged from that awful place.

I had not been in this new situation for very long before I realised that I had again received a posting that most soldiers could only dream about. Each weekend was free for the officers who required to be transported to Positano (situated between Sorrento and Amalfi) where they would relax in the comfort of a hotel. The drivers were accommodated in quite comfortable conditions in an old requisitioned house, high up on the hillside, overlooking the town and the sea.

From our new weekend home I looked down on Positano and gasped. At that magic moment the beautiful coastline, the deep blue sea, and the colour of the picturesque little town combined to provide a picture of paradise! It was not long before we were in early spring and the weather was improving each day. The busy weekend routine kept us fully occupied and time went swiftly by. The weekends were a joy. On one beautiful Sunday morning, relaxing with friends on the little beach, my thoughts went back to the long hard war years and the suffering still being endured world-wide by millions in the aftermath of the war. I knew that it would soon be time for me to be demobilised and to return home to an uncertain future in an England still enduring rationing, austerity and the tail end of a bitterly cold winter. I had longed for the day when I could return home but now, in these idyllic circumstances, I was in no hurry! I had established a friendly relationship with the Officer in Charge (Group Captain Selby). I explained my views to him and received an encouraging response.

"Gianotti, you're doing a good job here and I don't want to lose you but you are due for demob any day now." He continued, "If you like I can arrange for you to stay on for another month or so which might suit us both."

I thanked him and agreed to sign on until the first week in May. I had been placed in charge of all transport details some time previously and decided that I would arrange matters so that the last month or so would be as enjoyable as possible for myself and the others. In all my army experience I had never been so much in control of my daily routine and the last weeks in Naples were the most carefree days I had ever experienced.

We made friends with Italian civilians in Naples, and especially in Positano and nearby Amalfi, where most evenings were spent in their company, usually in little bars where Neapolitan music was played, creating a wonderfully relaxing Southern Italian atmosphere. In Positano I spent some time also in the company of the army officers, often enjoying a drink with them in the bar of their hotel, and I began to develop a taste for the good life that they so obviously enjoyed. I knew that to improve my position in civilian life I would need to get back to my job in England without further delay.

The idyll finally came to an end on May 9th 1947 when I returned to my unit in Padova. Before leaving I was given a Letter of Commendation from Group Captain Selby, a most unusual occurrence in the army (I still have it, all these years later). The letter serves as a reminder of a joyous, all too brief, period of my army life.

56. The Long Journey Home

The remaining days spent in Padova were to be the last days of my long period of army service in Italy and I found myself reflecting on all the things that had happened to me during that time, including many experiences about which I have not written.

I thought also of the great friendships I had developed with so many of my comrades, in particular with my closest friends, Sid Riley and Arthur Watcham.

On the last evening in Padova I arranged to have a last drink with them and as many of my friends as possible. Although there was the bright prospect of my return to England and civilian life, saying a final farewell to friends that I had known for so long left me with a feeling of great sadness. It was very difficult for me to accept that this part of my life had finally come to an end.

The long journey home was very uncomfortable. I was first taken by truck to Milan with a few other soldiers who were returning home. In Milan we boarded a train, packed absolutely full of soldiers bound for England on what was part of the MEDLOC route (Middle East direct line of communications). It was a journey that was to take almost two days, first in a packed railway carriage with occasional stops at what were quaintly described as 'feeding halts'! At these halts we received hot food of very doubtful quality from steaming vats. This was ladled into our mess tins and consumed by the side of the train. To obtain some relief from the cramped conditions in the railway carriage, and having the advantage of being small, I managed to claim a position on one of the luggage racks where I was able to rest and even to sleep a little. The train's progress was very slow. From Milan it passed through the town of Novara and then turned north towards Lake Maggiore where there were some wonderful views of the lake with it's many lovely islands. I enjoyed this part of the journey as much as I was able to in the cramped conditions. The train chugged on through Domodossola, passing through Switzerland and the towns of Brig, Martigny and Lausanne. After many delays and halts we gradually made our way through France, passing Valorbes, Digon, Sens, Paris and Amiens. Then, finally, through Abbeville and Boulogne to Calais. Here we left the train and spent the night in an army transit camp. The train journey had left me feeling very tired and stiff in every limb and even an old palliasse on a hard wooden bed offered heavenly comfort for my last night abroad.

The following morning I crossed the English Channel on a crowded troopship and experienced the thrill of seeing the lovely English coastline. Everything looked very beautiful.

Finally I was back home in England.

57. A Civilian Again!

On May 21st 1947 the day for my demobilisation finally arrived and I found myself at the barracks in Aldershot, undergoing the last rites of army life. First there was a medical examination in which I was graded 'A1', then all manner of documentary proceedings and, finally, the issuing of every soldier's entitlement – the civilian clothes in which to depart from the army. The issue consisted of a two-piece suit and a raincoat, shoes and various other items of civilian clothing. I had the usual problem of finding garments that fitted but eventually emerged looking fairly well turned out. I was given the final travel pass to cover the journey home.

As I left the barracks my feelings were very mixed; for over 4½ years I had been a soldier, always in the company of other men. Once I had adapted to army life I had never experienced any difficulty in getting along with my comrades and, despite the rigours of army life, there were many things that made it tolerable:- three meals a day were always provided, also clothing and a place in which to sleep. The pay was very low but generally sufficient to cover basic needs. Above all I had always had the feeling of being protected by the army and by my fellow soldiers. I had, as it were, for the major part of my army life, lived in a cocoon. Now, suddenly, I was absolutely alone again. It all seemed very strange to me and I knew I would need time to settle down to civilian life again. However, any fears that I may have had were swiftly dispelled.

Now I was a free man again. I could get back to my family and my business and plan my life ahead. In the army I had learned to cope with all kinds of different situations and learned how to deal with different people. The confidence gained would be beneficial in the years ahead. I reflected how fortunate I had been. I had experienced things in wartime that many would not normally experience in a lifetime; I had returned home unscathed and was still only 23 years of age. All these thoughts occupied my mind during the journey home.

When I finally arrived, my mother was waiting for me. She embraced me warmly and wept. My brothers, David and Ted, were now both away on military service and my arrival, therefore, was timely. When I had settled down and had a bath I opened a bottle of wine brought home for the occasion and we chatted for hours.

It was great to be home again.

58. Back to Italy

After a day or so at home, gradually re-adjusting to civilian life again, I called to see my employers who were still operating from Regency House in Warwick Street. It seemed very strange to be back in central London, after such a long period, and I did not enjoy the journey in a crowded smoke-filled underground train. There were a few new faces in the office and also some of the staff that I had known before the war. They all greeted me very warmly and the managing director took me to lunch. It was agreed that I would finish the whole of my demobilisation leave and return to work on the 21st of July.

On the journey home I decided that this would be a perfect opportunity for me to take my mother to Italy. I had received a sum of money as a gratuity and as soon as I got home I told her what I proposed to do. She was overjoyed although a little apprehensive about the short notice. We decided to leave in about a week and I got busy arranging for passports, booking the travel and, of course, writing to my Uncle Giovanni in Milan. I had received an open invitation from him when last in Turin and knew that there would be no problem at the Italian end.

In just a week we were on our way. The journey was very tiring – by train to Dover, then the ferry to Ostend, then by train again on the long overnight route to Milan, passing through Brussels in Belgium. I had not been able to afford first-class travel and the train journey was spent sitting in a carriage which was full, on uncomfortable seats. My mother was marvellous – never a word of complaint and a smile for everybody on the train.

After what seemed an eternity we reached Milan and we travelled by tram to Viale Monte Nero. The welcome we received from my Uncle Giovanni, his sister-in-law and her son Ottavio was as I expected. They virtually overwhelmed us, smothering us with embraces and kisses while weeping for the joy of the occasion. When things had calmed down a little we were given a splendid lunch during which everybody chatted incessantly. Afterwards we enjoyed a siesta which lasted about two hours. We were both absolutely sold out!

During the days that followed Ottavio showed us all the places of interest in Milan and we were able to meet Constantino Pallavidini. He arranged to take us to the Scala Opera House where we enjoyed the wonderful spectacle of an opera performed magnificently in a marvellous setting.

"Frank," my mother remarked, when the performance was over, "this has been the most wonderful evening of my life".

After all the hardships she had endured that reaction was understandable.

After our short stay in Milan we travelled by train to Turin and, again, the reception was fantastic. My cousin Gina once more organised everything and my mother's joy at meeting my father's brothers and sisters once again knew no bounds. We visited all the places she had seen with my father over twenty years before and she recalled, happily, events that had taken place at that time. She loved Turin and was very reluctant to leave that beautiful city but inevitably we had to move on to Ivrea for the last days of our holiday. No bicycle ride this time, my cousin Giovanni took us by car. Again, we received a rapturous welcome from my aunt and uncle and my two cousins. Our accommodation at Uncle Guido's home was luxurious and we enjoyed a very relaxed spell in Ivrea.

The peaceful nature of this part of our holiday was rudely disturbed by one very unusual event. On the second night in Ivrea my mother, who was sleeping in a room next to mine, was awakened by sounds of breaking glass; she called out to me "Frank, what is happening?" I had been in a deep sleep but swiftly collected my wits and listened. There was the sound of torrential rain beating on the roof and at the same time I could hear crashing sounds and the shattering of glass. I went to the window and looked out – to my astonishment I could see big pieces of ice falling into the street below and bouncing off in every direction. There was obviously some kind of storm going on and in just a few minutes this increased in intensity until the sound reached a crescendo. It was a frightening noise – just as if we were under bombardment!

"Don't worry mum," I called out, "It's just a storm".

"I've never heard a storm like this," she replied, "perhaps it's the end of the world". She was prone to letting her imagination run riot occasionally but I could understand her thinking at that moment.

"Don't worry you silly old thing," I said, "It will all be over soon enough". I was right, after about two minutes the din abated. By now all the members of the family were awake and in a state of apprehension. I put on some clothes and went outside into the street. There were shattered windows and roofs, with broken glass everywhere and people inspecting the damage caused. There was little to be achieved at that moment and we returned to our beds.

The following morning my Uncle Guido's glass factory was besieged by people urgently needing repairs to windows and glass doors. It was quite chaotic! It had been a freak mountain storm, more severe than they had ever experienced before, and almost everybody in the town seemed to have been affected in one way or another. I decided that it would be a relief for the family if we were out of the way while they coped with the situation and I took mother out for the day.

After the excitement caused by the storm the ensuing days were spent quietly enjoying the local lakes and beautiful mountain walks. Finally we reached the end of our holiday and once again had to say goodbye and return to England. The journey home was uneventful and we both quietly reflected on the superb fortnight that we had enjoyed. Again I felt immense gratitude for the kindness and love showered upon us by my Italian family.

Back home again I realised that I had spent my entire gratuity in two weeks. I had no regrets whatsoever; never had money been so well spent. My mother's complete happiness throughout the whole fortnight had given me more pleasure and satisfaction than I could possibly have imagined. Now I would have to get back to being the provider, earning my living again in a manner to which I had become unaccustomed.

59. I Return to Civilian Life

On July 21st 1947 I started my career in advertising again. It seemed strange to be making my way to work on the underground train and even stranger when I reached my office. I had been provided with a desk in fairly comfortable surroundings, in a room occupied by two other men, and I knew that it would be a while before I adjusted fully to a completely different lifestyle. I had been away for nearly five years. I gazed at my clean blotter and new note pads and chuckled to myself as I recalled the words of that great journalist 'Cassandra', exquisitely describing his feelings in the same situation, after the same five year absence:

"Now where was I when I was so rudely interrupted?"

It did not take long before I got into my stride – the media department of the agency was almost non-existent and I was given the task of reorganisation. Having an orderly mind this did not pose any great problems and there was the bonus of being able to escape from the office periodically to meet representatives from the advertising departments of the national and provincial newspapers. I became familiar with the numerous pubs and restaurants in the West End and in Fleet Street in particular and revelled in the atmosphere of that famous street – then the hub of the newspaper world.

The owner of the business also ran a small export company and I was asked to devote part of my time to assist in the day to day running of this enterprise. This business did not survive for long but I acquired some knowledge of export and shipping procedures and generally expanded my knowledge of commerce outside advertising, all of which was to be very helpful in later years.

The complete transformation from army to civilian life took place very quickly and I decided that I would enjoy my new found freedom and make up for the years of my youth lost to the war. I joined a sports club in South London, mainly consisting of young men demobilised from the armed forces, and played cricket in summer and football in the winter months. These carefree activities, and the social life accompanying them, were interspersed with watching county cricket (in particular the magnificent batting of Denis Compton and Bill Edrich for Middlesex) and making regular visits to Highbury to enjoy the outstanding successes of Arsenal in the football world.

Conditions were still very difficult and rationing continued for some time after the end of the war but, despite the austerity that the country still had to endure, the years from 1947 to 1951 were, for me, golden years of great happiness. My brothers eventually came home after completing military service in the army and in 1951 we moved to a large apartment in Sydenham Hill. My dear mother rejoiced – the family was united again.

In the early part of 1951 management decided that I needed a secretary and I interviewed a young lady, Margaret Ashby, only 18 years of age. I was impressed by the smart appearance and cheerful manner of this attractive young girl and signed her on despite her lack of experience. I felt that I would be able to work well with her and it proved to be so. During the ensuing months we worked long hours together and became good friends. I did not know then that she would play a major role in my life in the years ahead.

60. Back in the Army

When all is going well in life you can be sure that something will happen to foul things up. So it was in September 1951. In my morning mail there was an official letter instructing me to report for 14 days army training, in early October, to Taunton in Somerset. I had known at the time of demobilisation in 1947 that I had been placed on 'Z' reserve and that a recall to the army was always a possibility, nevertheless the letter came as something of a shock. There was no escaping the training course and, on the appointed day, I made my way to Taunton and reported to the army barracks there. Also reporting were a good many men of about my own age all cursing at having their lives interrupted again after lengthy wartime service. It was inevitable, however, and the general attitude was that it would be sound policy to get on with it – treat the whole thing as a lark, and enjoy it as much as possible!

The conditions at the barracks were quite good by army standards and the food edible. After a couple of days of the usual drills and some time spent on the firing range I found myself at the wheel of a three-ton truck again, driving in convoys through the very pleasant county of Somerset. It all seemed very unreal but, at least for this short time, the lifestyle was not too difficult to tolerate. The training course was an unwelcome interruption of my business affairs but a good spirit of comradeship existed and it was interesting to see again how men from so many different walks of life could be so swiftly welded into an efficient unit. At the end of the course the whole group was transported to Weston-Super-Mare for a day off – it turned out to be a glorious binge!

Before departing from the barracks for the journey back home each man was informed that his kit would be individually boxed and labelled in readiness for any future national emergency. The response from each man to the duty sergeant issuing this information followed a regular pattern, mostly advising him, somewhat indelicately, where these boxes might be deposited!

Just before leaving I was handed a postcard sent by my colleagues at the office, on which various good luck messages were scrawled. At the end of the postcard was written "Lots of love, Margaret", followed by a few kisses. Somehow these few words struck a chord. At that moment I realised that I had become very fond of her and was missing her cheerful company and warm smile. I had not previously ventured to ask her out for an evening after work, perhaps deterred by the ten-year difference in our ages. I would do so as soon as possible after returning home.

61. Black Friday – February 29th 1952

I left my office early on Friday evening and took the underground train from Piccadilly Circus to the Elephant and Castle, stopping for a glass of Guinness at the famous pub on the corner, before taking the overhead train to Sydenham Hill. I felt elated. Nearly five years had passed since my demobilisation from the Army, my business prospects were beginning to look rosier and the winter was nearly over – with the promise of a season of cricket ahead. Above all my friendship with my little secretary seemed to be blossoming into something much deeper.

Upon arrival at Sydenham Hill station I walked the short distance to the estate in which our newly built flat was situated. As I neared the flat I sensed that there was something wrong. Normally upon arriving home there would be one or two people about – this evening I saw nobody and there was an almost uncanny silence. I quickened my step to reach home. Before I could insert my key in the lock the front door was opened. My two brothers were standing together in the hall, both looking deadly white. David came forward and put his hand on my shoulder. His voice choked with emotion, "Sorry Frank, I'm afraid there's bad news". "What's happened?" I replied, sensing something dreadful. "It's Mum," he said, "I'm afraid there's been an accident" and then, after a pause that was indescribably painful, "She's dead".

I was stunned. I could not immediately accept the awful reality. My recollections of the ensuing hours are hazy. My brothers explained that she had been struck in the back by a reversing electric milk float in a quiet courtyard on the estate.

She had died in the ambulance on the way to hospital. We wept but gained comfort from being together.

When I had regained my composure I had to face the painful duties that follow a death. We went together to Gypsy Hill Police Station where I collected my mother's possessions. The duty sergeant was very kind. "She didn't suffer, Sir." "It was all over very quickly". I could not bring myself to utter anything in reply. "I'm afraid you will have to go to the hospital for formal identification", he said.

At Dulwich Hospital we were taken to the mortuary. Both David and Ted preferred me to continue alone. I agreed that it would be best. I was taken to a room where my dear mother was laid on a bed. She was completely wrapped in white linen. Her skull had been crushed and her head was heavily bandaged. I was therefore denied one last glimpse of that sweet face. I knelt by her side and held her hand – the icy cold hand of death – the hand of the woman who had given me life. In the ensuing minutes I recalled how she had seen two World Wars. How she had endured the years of bombing in the last – bravely and alone. How she had brought up her three sons unaided after the premature death of my father and been such a shining example to us. How, despite every hardship, she had never complained and always had complete faith in God. I recalled how, only a few days before, she had returned joyously from a walk in Dulwich Park saying how happy she had been in the few months that she had been in our new home. She had been, for the first time in her life, free from worry and enjoying life's comforts so long denied to her. It seemed so cruel that this gentle soul should have had her life taken away so suddenly and so violently.

I said the Lord's Prayer and then my last goodbye. As I departed, blinded by my tears, a kindly orderly took my hand,

"Be strong – it was God's will", he said. I knew that they would have been her own words.

Thus ended the life of my beloved mother, Emily Violet Gianotti. For the rest of my life I would remember her daily with love and gratitude.

62. The End Of The Beginning

In the weeks following the death of my mother I felt a great sense of loss and suffered a period of depression. My brothers were similarly affected. We decided that the best course for us, at least in the immediate future, would be to continue to live together in Sydenham Hill in our comfortable apartment.

One of our neighbours, a Mrs Gregory – married with children, lived in an apartment on the ground floor below us. She was anxious to be of assistance and pleased to have the opportunity to increase her income by working for us for a few hours each day. Accordingly we arranged for her to do our shopping and to do some cleaning in the apartment. She would also occasionally prepare an evening meal for us.

The arrangement worked well and the three of us continued with our lives and our careers as our dear mother would have wished. During these months I saw Margaret frequently. She came to the apartment regularly, was warmly received by both David and Ted and was well liked by both of them. As the days passed by we became ever closer and I knew that this was the girl with whom I wanted to spend the rest of my life. I proposed, was accepted, and after a period of engagement we were married on July 25th 1953 in a little church in North London. Margaret was not yet 20 years of age and I had been apprehensive about the ten-year gap between our ages. My fears were groundless. It was to be a perfect marriage, based on love, mutual respect and understanding and we were later to be blessed with two fine sons.

My marriage provided the motivation for me to intensify my efforts in the advertising agency business. Now, in the second half of the 20th century, in a rapidly changing world, I saw that my life was entering a new phase. My wartime travels had thrown me into contact with people from every walk of life and I had gained a good understanding of human nature. Helped by this knowledge I had developed techniques for the most efficient use of the printed word in mail order advertising and had already begun to establish something of a reputation in that specialist field of advertising. I was not yet thirty years of age, was ambitious, and knew that I now had to expand my knowledge of all aspects of advertising and to use the good client contacts I had as a springboard to achieving my ambition – to form my own advertising agency.

By the grace of God (and a very large amount of good luck) I had survived the poverty of the thirties and the long years of war and emerged strengthened by my experiences, just as steel is hardened in a furnace. In this second stage of my life, encouraged by the love and constant support of my dear Margaret, I was to achieve my ambition.

In a career that was to be demanding, exciting, full of risks, and not without intrigue, the boy from Soho would ultimately realise his dream .... but that's another story!

63. An Extraordinary Coincidence

I had been endeavouring for a long period to find the name of the author of 'The Battle of Naseby', a poem that I had learned at school over sixty years previously. On February 10th 2000, together with my wife, I visited our local library to collect a book of war poems which, I had been informed, contained this poem.

When my wife gave her name (Gianotti) to the librarian a woman in the queue, accompanied by her husband, observed "Gianotti! That's an Italian name". "Yes, my husband's father was Italian" replied my wife. "We are also of Italian origin" said the woman, "Our name is Stratta". I realised then that we had seen this charming couple at Sunday morning mass in the little church at Rose Green, although we had never actually spoken to them.

The conversation that followed was intensely interesting to all concerned. I related some details of my life, including the locating of my Italian relatives in Italy as a soldier in the invading British army in 1945. Mr Stratta told of his own harrowing experiences – being taken prisoner in Calais at the time of the evacuation from Dunkirk, and spending long years as a prisoner of the Germans, in a prison camp in Poland.

Eventually I enquired "Where did you live before you came to Aldwick?" "Various places," said Mr Stratta, "But I originally lived in Soho, London, as did my wife Ida, then my childhood friend". I, also, had lived in Soho as a young boy and, becoming intrigued, asked a number of questions. To my amazement it transpired that the three of us had lived in the same apartment buildings in the same street (then called Little Pulteney Street) and attended the same school!

We could not recall having met, probably because I was about three years younger, but we had clear joint recollections of the names and the personalities of teachers, other pupils, local inhabitants and the unique nature of life in Soho at that time.

By now these discoveries had caused the conversation to become very animated and the tranquillity of the library was being seriously threatened! We decided, therefore, that we would meet briefly, after Sunday mass, on the following Sunday.

On the Sunday morning, after the mass had finished, we met outside the church and greeted each other warmly. I had one question yet to ask: "Tell me, Mr Stratta, what was the number of your apartment in the buildings?" He replied without hesitation, "Number 53". I gasped, I could hardly believe what I had heard.

It was the very same apartment in which I had lived with my family for about six years from 1929 – over 70 years ago!

We subsequently established that his family had vacated the apartment as my family moved in! A fantastic coincidence – or fate perhaps?

In any event our chance meeting had, for all of us, revived many memories of a bygone age.

Sadly, in September 2000 Candido Stratta died. In the short period since we met I had developed a firm friendship with this charismatic man. I am grateful for having known him and for the memories of my early years that our meeting had awakened.

~ END ~

Italy, August 1945 – the Author in convoy – Naples to Ancona.

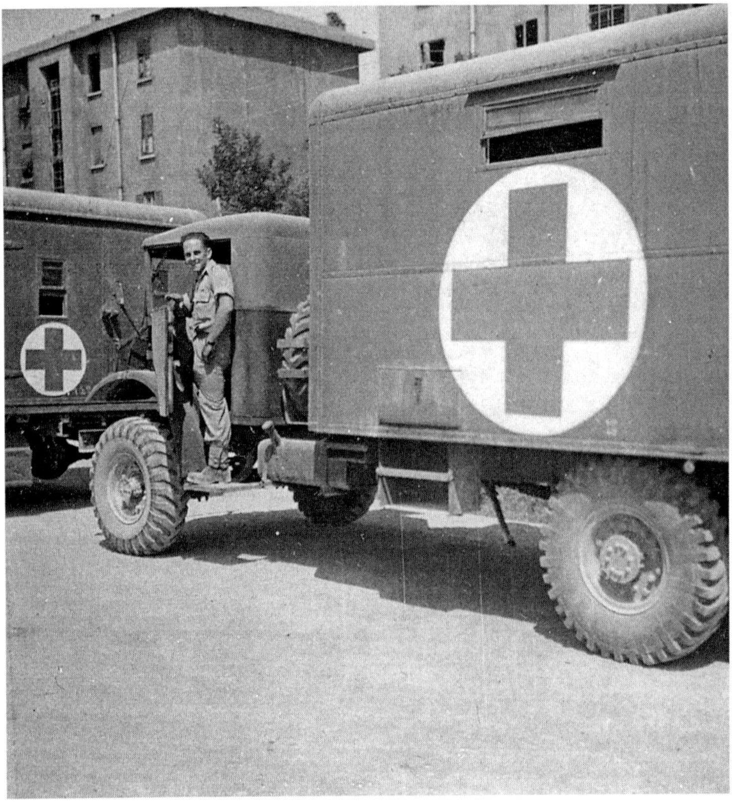

Ancona, July 1945 – ambulance driver.

Author's own photograph of the remains of Monte Cassino after the bombardment.

The Author – Like a DUKW to water!

August 1945 – the crew of the' Italia Liberata'.

A deadly cargo ready for disposal in the Adriatic on board the 'Italia Liberata'.

July 1946 – Two mules in the back of my truck for delivery to Naples.

Front row (from left) Frank, Ted and David Gianotti.